LEARNING TO PRAY
GOD'S WAY

LEARNING TO PRAY GOD'S WAY

DALE A. SCADRON, TH.D., D.D.

Learning to Pray God's Way - Copyright © 2024 by Dale Scadron. All rights reserved. No part of this publication may be reproduced, distributed, or transmitted in any form or by any means, including photocopying, recording, or other electronic or mechanical methods, without the prior written permission of the copyright owner and the publisher, except in the case of brief quotations embodied in critical reviews and certain other noncommercial uses permitted by copyright law. For permission requests, write to the publisher.
Chaplains College School of Graduate Studies,
13061 Rosedale Hwy. G-141. Bakersfield, CA 93314
/dr.dale@chaplainscollege.education / (888) 627-5503

Publishing Information:

CHAPLAINS COLLEGE PRESS

Printed in the United States of America.

INDEX

Chapter 1 - Unlocking the Power of Christian Prayer
Chapter 2 - Praying and Obeying
Chapter 3 - How to Effectively Pray in the Spirit
Chapter 4 - Praying with Thanksgiving
Chapter 5 - Why Our Prayers Lack Power?
Chapter 6 - Allowing God to Lead/Transform Your Life
Chapter 7 - Harnessing Prayer for Strength and Courage
Chapter 8 - Understanding the Lord's Prayer
Chapter 9 - Praying the Psalms
Chapter 10 - Standing Firm on God's Promises
Chapter 11 - The Power of Intercessory Prayer
Chapter 12 - Embracing the Role of a Prayer Warrior
Chapter 13 - Recognizing God's Answer to Prayer
Chapter 14 Unlocking the Power of the Prayer of Jabez

Chapter 1
Unlocking the Power of Christian Prayer

As we journey through our relationship with Christ, prayer serves as the bridge that enables us, flawed individuals, to communicate with God. It is a sacred conversation that goes beyond the confines of the physical world, allowing us to tap into God's boundless wisdom and love. Through prayer, we unleash a transformative force that reshapes our lives, rejuvenates our souls, and strengthens our bond with God. It sincerely expresses our innermost thoughts, aspirations, and struggles. Prayer is a dialogue with the One who knows us better than we know ourselves, inviting us to open our hearts and seek guidance, fortitude, and serenity.

When we engage in conversation with God, we open ourselves to the workings of the Holy Spirit, inviting a spiritual transformation that can impact every aspect of our lives. Prayer can heal emotional wounds, dissolve fears, and instill a sense of purpose and direction. It is a catalyst for personal growth and a means to cultivate virtues such as patience, humility, and compassion.

Spiritual transformation is a journey that requires us to release our perspectives and limitations. It entails shedding the layers of ego, fear, and doubt that obscure our true nature and impede our connection with Christ. Through spiritual transformation, we realize that our lives are not solely physical experiences but spiritual journeys.

Spiritual transformation is a continual process of growth, evolution, and refinement rather than a one-time event. It involves being open to letting go of old patterns, beliefs, and habits that no longer serve our highest good. It requires a commitment to self-reflection and introspection and a strong desire to align our thoughts, words, and actions with the will of God.

WHAT IS CHRISTIAN PRAYER?

Christian prayer is, at its core, a heartfelt conversation with the Triune God—the Father, the Son, and the Holy Spirit. It is a sacred exchange acknowledging our dependence on the Creator and our desire to align our lives with His will.

Through prayer, we express gratitude, confess our sins, intercede for others, and seek wisdom and understanding. It is a powerful means of surrendering our burdens and a comforting way to seek solace amidst life's storms.

"Prayer is the raising of one's mind and heart to God or the requesting of good things from God." - St. John Damascene

TYPES OF CHRISTIAN PRAYER

The rich tapestry of Christian prayer encompasses various forms, each serving a unique purpose and offering a distinct pathway to connect with God. Here are some of the most common types of Christian prayer:

1. **Adoration:** This prayer expresses awe, reverence, and worship towards God. It acknowledges His greatness, majesty, and sovereignty and often involves using psalms, hymns, and spiritual songs.
2. **Confession:** Confession is humbly acknowledging our sins and shortcomings before God. It recognizes our imperfections and requests forgiveness and cleansing.

3. **Thanksgiving:** Gratitude is at the heart of this type of prayer, where we express our appreciation for the blessings and provisions bestowed upon us by God's grace.
4. **Supplication:** Also known as petitionary prayer, supplication involves making requests to God for our needs, the needs of others, or specific situations. It is a way of casting our cares upon the Lord and seeking His divine intervention.
5. **Intercession:** This form of prayer involves standing in the gap for others, lifting their needs, struggles, and circumstances before the throne of grace.
6. **Praise:** Praise is a joyful expression of worship and adoration, celebrating God's attributes, works, and character.
7. **Meditation:** In this type of prayer, we ponder and reflect on the Word of God, allowing it to penetrate our hearts and transform our minds.
8. **Contemplation:** Contemplative prayer involves quieting our minds and hearts, creating space for stillness, and listening to the gentle whispers of the Holy Spirit.

These diverse forms of prayer offer us ways to engage with Christ in conversations. Each serves a unique purpose and caters to our spiritual journey's various needs and seasons.

BENEFITS OF ENGAGING CONVERSATIONS

Engaging in divine conversations through prayer offers many benefits that can impact our lives and spiritual well-being. Here are some of the transformative advantages of embracing a vibrant prayer life:

1. **Deepening our Relationship with God:** Prayer is the lifeblood of our connection with God. Through regular communication, we cultivate intimacy, trust, and a deeper understanding of God's character and will for our lives.
2. **Receiving Guidance:** Amid life's complexities and uncertainties, prayer provides a channel for seeking wisdom, direction, and clarity from the ultimate source of truth.
3. **Experiencing Inner Peace and Joy:** Prayer can calm our restless souls, soothe our

anxieties, and fill us with a profound sense of peace and joy that transcends circumstances.

4. **Cultivating Spiritual Growth:** As we engage in divine conversations, we open ourselves to the transformative work of the Holy Spirit, allowing our minds and hearts to be renewed and our character to be refined.
5. **Strengthening Faith and Trust:** Prayer is an exercise in relinquishing control and placing our lives in the hands of the One who knows us best. It fosters a deeper trust in God's sovereignty and ability to work all things for our ultimate good.
6. **Interceding for Others:** Prayer allows us to stand in the gap for others, lifting their needs, struggles, and circumstances before the throne of grace and becoming vessels of God's love and compassion.
7. **Spiritual Empowerment**: Through prayer, we tap into the limitless power of the Holy Spirit, enabling us to overcome challenges, resist temptations, and triumph over the forces of darkness.

These benefits are not mere promises but tangible realities that countless believers have experienced throughout the ages. As we commit to a life of prayer, we open ourselves to the transformative power of divine conversations, which can reshape our lives and propel us toward a more profound, more fulfilling spiritual journey.

Chapter 2
Praying and Obeying

In our faith journey, we discover that the fundamental principles guiding our spiritual path are deeply rooted in scriptures about obedience. Obedience, as portrayed in various scriptures, is not merely about submission but is an expression of our trust and love for Christ. This concept is central in spiritual life and is the foundation for our relationship with God and our understanding of prayer and faith.

As we explore the importance of obedience to God, we will also confront the challenges that often impede our path to obedience and share practical steps to overcome these hurdles.

Obedience, in the Biblical sense, is not just about compliance but a deep-rooted expression of faith and reverence toward God. It involves hearing and acting upon God's word, aligning our will to His. This concept is vividly illustrated through Christ's example, as He became obedient even to the point of death. The Bible emphasizes that obedience is our duty, reflecting a submissive compliance to God's authority.

OBEDIENCE AND GOD'S LOVE

Our obedience is an act of love towards God. It demonstrates our trust in His goodness and our commitment to follow His lead, even when outcomes are uncertain. This relationship is underscored by Jesus' words, "If you love me, keep my commands," linking obedience directly with love. Obedience is not only about following orders but is a heartfelt response to God's love for us.

We demonstrate our utmost love and reverence for Him by obeying God's commands. This act of obedience becomes a worshipful offering, showcasing that we prioritize God's will above our desires. As we walk in obedience, we engage in an ongoing act of worship that glorifies God and deepens our relationship with Him.

Prayer is not just a means to align our hearts with God's will; it is a powerful demonstration of our trust and surrenders to His perfect plan. This alignment strengthens our resolve to obey and deepens our understanding of God's desires over our own. The act of praying with faith is not just an acknowledgment of God's sovereignty but an invitation for His guidance and strength to enter our lives, making obedience not just a goal but a secure and guided path.

The Holy Spirit plays a crucial role in being obedient. By revealing God's truth and wisdom through Scripture, the Spirit empowers us to live by God's will. As we pray, the Spirit works within us, transforming our hearts and minds to foster a more profound commitment to obedience. This divine assistance is essential for us to carry out God's commands faithfully and with joy.

In prayer, we seek to communicate with God and receive the strength to obey His commands. Prayer is a powerful way to express our dependence on God for the ability to live righteously. In these moments of heartfelt prayer, we are most open to the transformative power of the Holy Spirit, which guides us toward a life of obedience.

IDENTIFYING COMMON BARRIERS TO OBEDIENCE

Obedience to God often presents challenges, including fear and guilt. Fear and guilt can paralyze us, preventing us from stepping out in faith and creating roadblocks in our prayer life and our relationship with God.

Prayer and scripture serve as powerful aids in overcoming barriers to obedience. Through prayer, we actively seek strength and courage to follow God's will, while scripture, a wellspring of wisdom and guidance, illuminates His commands. By immersing ourselves in these spiritual practices, we align our hearts with God's desires. This alignment empowers us to conquer fear, pride, and personal plans that deviate from His purposes, leading us to a deeper, more fulfilling relationship with Him.

LIVING A LIFE OF OBEDIENCE

We start with simple, daily practices to build a life of obedience. Listening to God's commandments and applying biblical teachings are foundational. This includes refraining from negative behaviors like gossip and embracing virtues such as patience and kindness. Regular engagement with Scripture is crucial, as it empowers us to make the right choices and resist temptation.

"We flourish not in obedience in isolation but within a community." Anonymous

Sharing our journey with others provides accountability, a sense of belonging, and support. As we interact and serve within our community, our collective commitment to God's commands strengthens, fostering a supportive environment for spiritual growth.

Christ is the ultimate example of obedience. Focusing on Him, understanding His teachings, and meditating on His life can inspire us to deepen our obedience. Keeping Christ at the center of our lives aligns us with God's will and allows His grace to transform us into obedient followers. This focus ensures that our actions comply with divine directives and glorify God in all aspects of our lives.

Throughout this chapter, we have untangled the intricate connection between obedience and faith, guided by the wisdom of Scripture. Obedience is a testament to our submission and a powerful declaration of our love and trust in Christ. We discovered how these elements guide us toward a life that harmonizes with God's will. The challenges that may obstruct our path remind us of the necessity for unwavering faith. The practical steps and insights we draw from the

Scriptures serve as a guiding light, illuminating the path to a life enriched by obedience.

At the core of this journey lies the example of Christ, whose life acts as a beacon, showing us how to embody obedience in all aspects of our being. Let us wholeheartedly embrace the call to obedience, understanding that our greatest strength and freedom come from submission rather than resistance.

Chapter 3

How to Effectively Pray in the Spirit

Praying in the Spirit is a spiritual practice that allows you to connect with God on a deeper level with the guidance of the Holy Spirit. In this chapter, we'll explore the role of the Holy Spirit in prayer, providing practical steps to help you pray in the Spirit effectively. We'll also discuss the numerous benefits of praying in the Spirit that will empower you to cultivate a more intimate relationship with God.

As a believer, your prayer life is intricately connected with the Holy Spirit. He is not just a distant figure but your helper and intercessor, guiding and shaping your prayers to align with God's will.

The Holy Spirit knows what you should pray. He intercedes for you with groanings too deep for words, presenting your prayers to God according to His will. The Spirit reminds you that you are a child of God, empowering you to approach the

Father boldly. By walking with the Spirit and allowing Him to lead you and grow His fruit in your life, your desires align with His. Your prayers expand from personal needs to God's kingdom, from seeking comfort to making disciples. The Spirit guides you into all truth, disclosing what belongs to Christ.

Praying according to God's will requires knowing His Word, which unveils His divine plan. By remaining connected to Christ and allowing His Word to dwell within you, you develop a deeper understanding of areas needing more remarkable Christlike resemblance. Whether relying on specific promises or general principles, praying by Scripture aligns your petitions with the heart of the Father.

CULTIVATING A SPIRIT OF DEPENDENCE AND SURRENDER

Understanding the power of prayer is not only life-changing; it brings you into God's presence, becoming a living act of fellowship and communion. You bow before God as a humbled child in awe, with an awakened sense of intimacy and wonderment.

Meditating on God's Word means marinating, mulling over, reflecting, dwelling on, and pondering the Scriptures, resulting in a transformative engagement with God. It's done quietly with God, empowered by the Holy Spirit, to replace your thinking with God's. As you meditate, you'll likely enter a dialogue with God through prayer, and the Lord will speak to you through His living Word and His Holy Spirit.

The Holy Spirit, a gentle guide, will direct your life as you learn to recognize and follow His promptings. These promptings are often quiet and subtle but bring peace to your mind. Instead of rushing after saying "amen," take a moment; stay on your knees and listen because the Lord might be trying to "speak peace to your mind". He offers you a moment of calmness and reassurance in your spiritual journey.

To persevere in prayer is to believe that all things are possible with God, to believe in God's purpose, and to accept His will. When we ask God for wisdom, we should do so with unwavering faith, for the one who doubts should not expect to receive anything from the Lord.

When you pray in the Spirit, you cultivate intimacy with God, allowing you to experience a deeper connection. As you converse with God through prayer, guided by the Holy Spirit, you gain access to a personal and fulfilling relationship. The Spirit enables you to share your innermost thoughts and desires with the Father, fostering a sacred bond that can only be felt in the depths of your heart.

When you pray in the Spirit, you are equipped with heightened spiritual sensitivity and the ability to discern God's voice. The Spirit enlightens your understanding, enabling you to clearly perceive spiritual truths and align your desires with God's perfect will. This spiritual discernment empowers you to navigate life's complexities with confidence and the wisdom that comes from above.

As you pray in the Spirit, your desires and prayers increasingly align with God's purposes and plans. The Holy Spirit intercedes on your behalf, shaping your prayers according to the Father's will. This alignment ensures that your requests are in harmony with God's overarching design, allowing you to participate in His divine agenda for your life and the world around you.

Praying in the Spirit equips you with the power and enablement necessary for spiritual growth and effective ministry. The Holy Spirit empowers you to proclaim the gospel boldly, operate in the gifts of the Spirit, and bear spiritual fruit that impacts those around you. As you yield to the Spirit's guidance through prayer, you become a vessel for God's transformative work in your life and the lives of others.

Chapter 4
Praying with Thanksgiving

Gratitude sanctifies our lives, allowing us to be genuinely receptive to the presence of Christ working within and around us—now. As we offer a sacrifice of praise through thankful lips, we acknowledge God's hand and remain focused on His work. The Bible urges us to pray with thanksgiving, presenting our requests to God with gratitude. This spirit of thanksgiving in prayer aligns with God's will and fills our minds with His unexplainable peace.

We are called to kneel in prayer, adorned with gratitude and a heart overflowing with thanksgiving. As we implore God's favor, placing our requests before Him like precious jewels on an altar of hopefulness, we embrace His divine will for us. In this sacred practice lies the key that unlocks inexplicable peace; when we wrap ourselves within its hallowed folds, our souls find utter contentment as they bask in the warmth of God's loving embrace.

When gratefulness is expressed with enthusiasm and sincerity, it serves as a mechanism to redirect our attention from obstacles toward the majesty of God. Incorporating moments for thanksgiving into personal devotion allows one to nurture hopefulness and tranquility within life's mundane experiences—indeed, a vital undertaking for spiritual well-being.

BIBLICAL COMMANDS ON GIVING THANKS

- The Bible encourages us to "give thanks in all circumstances, for this is God's will. (1 Thessalonians 5:18) *"Give thanks in all circumstances; for this is God's will for you in Christ Jesus." (NASB)*
- We are called to "continually offer up a sacrifice of praise...the fruit of lips that give thanks. (Hebrews 13:15) *"Through Him, then, let us continually offer up a sacrifice of praise to God, that is, the fruit of lips that give thanks to His name." (NASB)*
- Thanksgiving aligns our prayers with God's sovereign will. (Psalm 100:4). "Enter His gates with thanksgiving *and* His courts with praise. Give thanks to Him, bless His name."

- When we express gratitude to God for His presence in our circumstances, not just for the circumstances themselves, it becomes a "sacrifice of thanksgiving" that shifts our perspective. Recounting God's redemption produces gratitude even in difficult times.

Even during challenging moments, there are still reasons to be grateful - a kind word, the beauty of nature, or life's simple comforts. Shifting our mindset to appreciate what we have rather than dwelling on what we lack enables us to perceive situations more positively. Expressing gratitude by writing a letter to someone who has supported us can be incredibly impactful.

Maintaining a gratitude journal to document daily blessings helps to foster a heart of gratitude. Beginning and ending our prayers with thanksgiving acknowledges God's goodness. Reflecting on Scripture passages about God's character and mighty acts inspires us to give thanks.

EXPERIENCING GOD'S PEACE

When we pray with thanksgiving, we exchange our worries for God's inexplicable peace that guards our hearts and minds. Thanksgiving is the voice of faith, expressing trust that God has heard and will answer our prayers. As we consistently thank Him, even before seeing the answer, His peace invades our circumstances.

STRENGTHENING OUR RELATIONSHIP WITH GOD

Thanksgiving brings us into God's presence, enabling us to draw near to Him. Expressing heartfelt gratitude heightens our perception of the Lord who loves and blesses us. Thanking God aligns our prayers with His will and leads us to experience His nearness intellectually and in our hearts.

DEVELOPING A JOYFUL HEART

God wants us to have a heart always filled with gratitude. Reflecting on His faithfulness and the blessings He has bestowed upon us can help us shift our negative thoughts into positive ones. We experience thankfulness when we recall His love for us, the care we receive from others, the things that enhance our lives, and the many other beautiful gifts from God. When we maintain a joyful and grateful heart, it brings happiness into our lives, too!

Fostering gratitude is more than a spiritual practice; it's a way of life that brings boundless joy and reinforces our faith in the Lord. By continually offering praises and reflecting on His wondrous deeds, our outlook is reshaped, allowing us to embrace the benefits of a grateful heart - a closer connection with God, an inner serenity that defies comprehension, and a joyful demeanor that emanates His light to those in our midst.

Chapter 5
Why Our Prayers Lack Power?

Prayer has the power to greatly impact our lives. It is a sacred practice that enables us to connect with God and seek guidance, strength, and solace in times of need. Despite prayer's immense inherent power, many people struggle to unlock its full potential. This chapter will examine why our prayers may lack influence on God and explore ways to cultivate more meaningful and transformative experiences through prayer.

When we approach prayer with sincerity, humility, and an open heart, we create a channel for God's grace to enrich our lives. Prayer is not just a recitation of words or a ceremonial act, but a profound expression of our innermost thoughts, desires, and emotions. It is through these essential elements that our prayers gain the power to connect with the sacred and manifest our desired outcomes, transforming our lives in the process.

Prayer is a personal journey unique to each individual. It is a sacred practice that holds transformative potential. By recognizing the common barriers that can hinder the power of our prayers, we can take steps to overcome them and unlock the unique transformative potential within this sacred practice tailored to our individual experiences.

Faith is the bedrock upon which the power of prayer rests. It is the unwavering belief that God will hear and answer our prayers. Without faith, our prayers may become mere words devoid of the spiritual energy and conviction necessary to manifest their intended outcomes.

When we approach prayer with sincere faith, our words resonate beyond the physical realm. We embrace infinite possibilities beyond our understanding, empowered by faith to release doubt and embrace God's wisdom.

It's crucial to grasp that faith is not a static state; it's a dynamic journey that calls for constant cultivation and nurturing. Regular prayer and meditation on the Word of God can deepen our faith and strengthen our relationship with God.

COMMON REASONS WHY PRAYERS MAY LACK POWER

One significant reason our prayers may lack power may be true sincerity and genuine intention. When we approach prayer merely as a ritual or a habitual act devoid of heartfelt emotion and earnest desire, our words will likely fail to resonate with God.

True prayer goes beyond mere ritual; it is an act of self-reflection and vulnerability. It demands that we lay bare our souls before God with unwavering honesty and the genuine expression of our deepest longings, fears, and aspirations.

When we pray with genuine intention, our words carry a potent energy that can transcend the boundaries of the physical realm. Our prayers become imbued with the power of our deepest desires and the conviction of our beliefs, creating a powerful resonance that can attract the manifestation of our intentions.

UNRESOLVED CONFLICTS/UNFORGIVENESS

Unresolved conflicts and harbored resentments not only hinder the power of our prayers, but they also create a barrier to God's grace and mercy. When we cling to grudges, anger, or unforgiveness towards others or ourselves, we inadvertently obstruct the path to our spiritual growth and connection with God.

Prayer is not just about asking for God's assistance; it is an opportunity for self-reflection and personal growth. When we come to worship with resentment or unforgiveness, we unintentionally limit our ability to connect with God.

Unlocking the full power of our prayers requires us to courageously confront and release any lingering negative emotions or resentments that may be holding us back. We must also embrace a spirit of forgiveness and free ourselves from past hurts. Doing so creates space for healing, transformation, and the abundant flow of God's grace into our lives.

DOUBT AND LACK OF BELIEF IN THE POWER OF PRAYER

Doubt is a natural human experience, but when it comes to prayer, it can be a formidable obstacle to unlocking its true power. Approaching prayer with skepticism or disbelief can hinder our connection with God.

Doubt can stem from various sources, such as past disappointments, negative experiences, or a lack of understanding of the spiritual realm. However, it is essential to recognize that doubt is a self-imposed limitation that can hinder our ability to connect with God and receive the blessings we seek. To overcome doubt, we must cultivate a mindset of openness, trust, and faith in God's wisdom and the power of prayer.

DISTRACTIONS/LACK OF FOCUS DURING PRAYER

In our fast-paced, modern world, it can be challenging to avoid distractions. Internal distractions, such as wandering thoughts, emotional turmoil, or physical discomfort, can hinder our prayer life and disrupt our fellowship with the Lord.

It's important to develop mindfulness and presence to address these distractions. This might involve creating a dedicated space for prayer, incorporating calming rituals or practices before engaging in prayer, or simply taking a few moments to quiet the mind and center ourselves before beginning our prayers.

PERSONAL GROWTH AND SPIRITUAL DEVELOPMENT

Prayer is not just a solitary act but a journey of personal growth and spiritual development. As we deepen our understanding of ourselves, our connection with the Lord, and our place in the extraordinary tapestry of existence, our prayers become imbued with greater depth, clarity, and power.

Embracing personal growth involves challenging our limiting beliefs, patterns, and behaviors to unlock our spiritual potential. It urges us to reflect, seek guidance, and cultivate compassion and humility.

SEEKING GUIDANCE AND INSPIRATION FROM SPIRITUAL LEADERS AND MENTORS

While prayer is a personal and intimate practice, seeking guidance and inspiration from spiritual leaders and mentors who have walked the path before us can be beneficial. Through their own experiences and spiritual wisdom, these individuals can offer invaluable insights and guidance on how to deepen our prayer practice and unlock its true power.

Spiritual leaders and mentors can impart techniques, practices, and perspectives to help us overcome the barriers that may hinder the efficacy of our prayers. They can guide us and help us cultivate a deeper connection with God. This journey of overcoming obstacles can lead to personal growth and strengthen our prayer life.

Being part of a spiritual community can provide a supportive environment where we can learn from others, share our experiences, and receive encouragement and accountability on our spiritual journey.

In conclusion, unlocking the secrets to powerful and meaningful prayers requires a multifaceted approach encompassing sincerity, faith, forgiveness, focus, personal growth, and spiritual development. By addressing the common barriers that may hinder the efficacy of our prayers and actively cultivating the qualities and practices that enhance their power, we can transform our prayer experience into a profound and transformative journey.

Chapter 6
Allowing God to Lead and Transform Your Life

There comes a time when we ask ourselves, "What is our purpose in life?" At these moments, we are reminded that God is in control and will lead us down the path that must be taken. It requires our submission to God without question.

Surrendering to God leads us into a realm overflowing with hope and possibilities, where God's boundless knowledge surpasses our limited human understanding. This act recognizes that our well-intentioned plans are just a tiny part of God's grand design for our lives. We access His wisdom and guidance by aligning our will with God's purpose.

Relinquishing our ambitions and desires to God is often mistaken for passive resignation, but it is, in fact, an active engagement with our faith. Trusting God's plan opens us up to peace and clarity, enabling us to navigate life's uncertainties confidently, knowing that a higher purpose is guiding our steps.

When we dedicate our will to God, we open ourselves to personal growth and resilience by nurturing deep and transformative trust. We find a sense of peace and security by entrusting our deepest hopes and fears to a loving parental figure with our best interests at heart. This act is not about giving up our autonomy but rather about making a conscious choice to align our paths with a divine direction that is believed to be wiser and more insightful than our own.

This form of spiritual surrender requires humility and a willingness to accept that we do not have all the answers. By doing so, we open ourselves up to personal growth. We begin to understand that obstacles and challenges are not merely setbacks but are opportunities for learning and development. Submitting our wills encourages a reflective state of mind where we can better understand our desires, motivations, and the greater purpose behind our experiences.

Moreover, this submission builds resilience. Knowing that someone greater is guiding us can provide comfort during hardship. It instills a sense of purpose and direction, even when the path ahead seems unclear. This perspective can transform our approach to life's trials, enabling us to confront adversity with courage and strength. By aligning our wills with God's direction, we gain a deeper understanding of ourselves and forge a stronger connection to the broader framework of existence. This alignment reveals our place in the grand design, paving the way to a more fulfilled and resilient life.

Fulfillment through this process comes from realizing that our lives are part of something greater than ourselves. We start to see that setbacks and challenges are not obstacles but opportunities for growth and lessons embedded within God plan. This shift in perspective can transform how we approach life's trials, making us more adaptable and resilient.

THE IMPORTANCE OF ALLOWING GOD TO LEAD
In a world that constantly bombards us with conflicting messages and societal pressures, allowing God to lead becomes a sanctuary for our souls. It is a refuge where we can find solace in the knowledge that our lives are not merely a product of chance, but a carefully crafted tapestry woven by the hand of God.

Allowing God to lead instills a profound sense of purpose and direction within us. We no longer wander aimlessly; instead, we walk with intention and conviction, guided by a force transcending our earthly limitations. This divine guidance grants us the strength and courage to navigate life's challenges, assured that we are never truly alone on this journey. Through this spiritual connection, we find solace and motivation, reinforcing our resolve to face adversities with unwavering faith. God's leadership transforms our lives, imbuing them with a deeper meaning and steadfast hope.

Through God's guidance, we are invited to confront our deepest fears and insecurities, to shed the layers of doubt and self-imposed limitations that have hindered our growth. It is a journey of self-discovery, where we come face-to-face with our true selves, stripped of the masks and pretenses we have worn for so long.

This divine journey often begins with a gentle nudge, a whisper in our hearts encouraging us to look deeper within. Through prayer, reflection, and meditation, we start to see beyond our constructed superficial layers. These layers often serve as defense mechanisms, hiding our vulnerabilities and shielding us from potential pain. However, under God's guidance, we find the courage to dismantle these barriers.

We might initially encounter discomfort and resistance as we peel back these layers. Once buried, our fears and insecurities rise to the surface and demand our attention. It is during these moments of vulnerability that we truly grow. We start recognizing the false beliefs and negative self-talk that have limited us. God's loving presence reassures us, reminding us that we are not alone in this process.

When we confront our fears, we begin to understand their origins. We trace back to past experiences, traumas, and moments of self-doubt that have shaped our current beliefs. This understanding is liberating. It enables us to release the grip these fears have on our lives. We move closer to our authentic selves with each layer we shed, experiencing a sense of freedom and empowerment.

This journey is not solely about removing negativity but also embracing our strengths and divine purpose. God's guidance illuminates our innate talents and potential. As we align more closely with our true selves, we begin to see the unique path for us. Though personal and distinct, this path is intertwined with a more excellent plan.

Confronting our deepest fears and shedding layers of doubt leads to profound transformation. We emerge more resilient, self-aware, and spiritually aligned. In this renewed state, we are better equipped to fulfill our purpose and contribute meaningfully to the world. Through God's unwavering guidance, we discover that our true selves are not defined by our fears but by our innate divine essence.

LETTING GO OF CONTROL AND TRUSTING IN GOD'S PLAN

Change is an inevitable part of life, often bringing about a complex process that demands the release of the familiar and an embrace of the unknown. This process is only sometimes comfortable; it may require us to let go of long-held beliefs, patterns, or relationships that no longer serve our highest good. Such attachments, though dear, can act as barriers to growth and progress.

Shedding these elements can be likened to a tree losing its leaves—while the immediate effect might be an appearance of barrenness, it is a precursor to growth and renewal. By letting go, we create a void that becomes fertile ground for new opportunities, perspectives, and experiences. This can be both daunting and liberating.

In this space of openness and potential, we can redefine our paths and align more closely with our true selves. By trusting the process, we allow room for personal evolution, cultivating resilience and adaptability. The change process, though fraught with uncertainty, leads to a richer, more fulfilling life experience.

Embarking on a journey of spiritual growth and personal transformation is an individual endeavor. It begins with the deliberate act of putting one foot forward and trusting God to lead the way. To take this first step, create moments of stillness in your daily life. These moments of quiet reflection and prayer provide a sanctuary where you can listen to the whispers of the Holy Spirit. Look for signs, feelings, or thoughts that resonate deep within your soul, as these may be messages from God guiding you toward your true purpose.

Your commitment to this path will transform your inner life and your interactions with the world around you. You'll find a greater sense of peace, purpose, and fulfillment as you align more closely with God's guidance.

Chapter 7
Harnessing Prayer for Strength and Courage

As we navigate the complexities of life, we have come to understand the transformative nature of prayer. It serves as a beacon of hope, illuminating the path forward and instilling a sense of resilience within us. Through prayer, we have learned to embrace the wisdom and strength that lies beyond our own limitations.

Throughout the Bible, we find numerous examples of individuals who harnessed the power of prayer to find strength and courage in the face of adversity. These stories are powerful reminders of the transformative nature of prayer and the unwavering faith that sustained those who sought solace in its embrace.

1. **Moses and the Parting of the Red Sea (Exodus 14:10-31):** When the Israelites found themselves trapped between the pursuing Egyptian army and the vast

expanse of the Red Sea, Moses prayed to God. Through his unwavering faith and fervent petitions, the waters miraculously parted, allowing the Israelites to cross to safety while their enemies were vanquished.

2. **Joshua and the Battle of Jericho (Joshua 6:1-27)**: Faced with the formidable walls of Jericho, Joshua sought guidance through prayer. God instructed him to have the Israelites march around the city for seven days, and on the seventh day, the walls came tumbling down, granting them victory through their faith and obedience.

3. **Daniel in the Lion's Den (Daniel 6:16-23)**: When Daniel was unjustly condemned to the lions' den for his unwavering faith, he turned to prayer for deliverance. Despite the grave danger, his prayers were answered, and he emerged unharmed, a testament to the power of faith and the protection granted through fervent prayer.

These biblical accounts are potent reminders that no matter how daunting the challenge or how insurmountable the odds may seem; prayer can unleash the strength and courage we need to overcome even the most formidable obstacles.

PRAYER TECHNIQUES FOR FINDING INNER STRENGTH

Prayer is not a one-size-fits-all practice; instead, it is a personal and intimate experience. As we embark on our journey of harnessing prayers for strength and courage, we must explore various techniques and find what resonates most profoundly with our souls. Here are some powerful prayer techniques that can help cultivate inner strength:

1. **Contemplative Prayer**: This prayer involves quieting the mind and entering deep stillness and presence. By letting go of distractions and focusing solely on God presence, we create space for inner peace and clarity to emerge, allowing us to draw upon our innate strength and resilience.
2. **Intercessory Prayer**: In this practice, we pray for and intercede on behalf of others, lifting their needs and concerns. By shifting our focus outward and cultivating compassion, we tap into a wellspring of

courage and strength that transcends our struggles.

3. **Scriptural Prayer**: We can craft our prayers using the powerful words and promises of sacred texts, drawing inspiration and guidance from them. This practice can deepen our faith and provide a profound connection to a rich spiritual heritage, empowering us with the strength and courage of those who came before us.

Regardless of our chosen technique, prayer is a powerful exercise in vulnerability and trust. By opening our hearts and minds to God, we create space for transformation, allowing us to tap into the boundless reservoir of strength and courage that lies within.

USING AFFIRMATIONS AND POSITIVE DECLARATIONS IN PRAYER

In addition to traditional prayer practices, incorporating affirmations and positive declarations can be a powerful tool for cultivating strength and courage. These affirmations remind us of our inherent worth, resilience, and God support surrounding us.

Affirmations can be woven into our prayers or stand alone as powerful statements of intention and self-empowerment. By repeating these positive declarations, we plant courage and strength within our minds and hearts, allowing them to take root and blossom into tangible manifestations of resilience.

Here are some examples of affirmations and positive declarations that can be incorporated into our prayers:

- "I am strong, capable, and courageous, for the Holy Spirit's presence dwells within me."
- "With faith as my guide, I fearlessly embrace the challenges before me."
- "I am protected, guided, and supported by a loving and compassionate God."
- "My strength is renewed with each breath, and my courage knows no bounds."
- "I am a warrior of light, and no obstacle can extinguish the flame of my determination."

As we navigate the complexities of life, the power of prayer stands as an unwavering beacon, guiding us through the darkest storms and illuminating the path toward strength and courage.

Throughout this journey, we have explored the transformative nature of prayer, from biblical examples of individuals who harnessed its power to overcome formidable obstacles to practical techniques and rituals that can deepen our connection with God. We have learned to incorporate affirmations, gratitude, and mindfulness into our practice, creating a holistic approach to cultivating inner fortitude.

Chapter 8
Understanding the Lord's Prayer

As believers, we are drawn to the beauty and timeless wisdom of the Lord's Prayer. This sacred Invocation, taught by Jesus Christ himself, has resonated through the ages, teaching us an important lesson when worshiping the Lord in prayer. In this exploration, we shall delve into the depths of this prayer, unveiling its profound meaning and transformative power in our lives.

The Lord's Prayer is a testament to the enduring connection between humanity and God. It serves as a bridge that spans the earthly and celestial realms, enabling us to commune with the Lord. Through its words, we are reminded of eternal truths that transcend time and space, inviting us to embrace the sacred within our beings.

As we embark on this journey, we shall uncover the layers of wisdom embedded within each phrase, revealing the profound lessons that have guided countless souls throughout the ages. Let us approach this exploration with open hearts and minds, ready to receive the Lord's Prayer's transformative power and integrate its teachings into our daily lives.

UNDERSTANDING THE STRUCTURE OF THE LORD'S PRAYER

The Lord's Prayer is a masterfully crafted composition, each line carefully woven to convey profound spiritual truths. Its elegant and purposeful structure guides us through reverence, surrender, and a deeper connection with God.

1. **The Invocation**: "Our Father, who art in heaven."
2. **The Reverence**: "Hallowed be thy name."
3. **The surrender**: "Thy kingdom come, thy will be done."
4. **The Petition**: "Give us this day our daily bread.
5. **The Reconciliation**: "Forgive us our trespasses, as we forgive those who trespass against us."
6. **The Guidance**: "Lead us not into temptation, but deliver us from evil."

Each component serves a unique purpose, weaving together a tapestry of spiritual wisdom that transcends the boundaries of faith and culture.

"OUR FATHER, WHO ART IN HEAVEN" REFLECTING ON THE NATURE OF GOD

The opening line of the Lord's Prayer immediately establishes a profound connection with God. By addressing God as "Our Father," we acknowledge the intimate relationship between the Creator and creation. This Invocation reminds us that we are not mere spectators in the cosmic drama but cherished children of God, embraced by an unconditional love that knows no bounds.

The phrase "who art in heaven" further deepens our understanding of God's nature. In this context, Heaven symbolizes the realm of the sacred, the dwelling place of the God. It reminds us that while God is ever-present and immanent in our lives, there exists a transcendent aspect that surpasses our finite comprehension.

Reflecting on this opening line invites us to cultivate a sense of awe and Reverence for God while simultaneously embracing the profound truth that we are intimately connected to the source of all creation.

"HALLOWED BE THY NAME": EXPLORING THE HOLINESS OF GOD

As we move deeper into the prayer, we encounter the phrase "Hallowed be thy name." This line invites us to contemplate the sacred nature of God and to honor the holiness that permeates every aspect of existence.

The word 'hallowed' carries a profound weight, conveying a sense of reverence and sanctity. It serves as a constant reminder that the name of God is not merely a label or a designation but a representation of the ineffable essence that transcends all human understanding. By hallowing the name, we acknowledge the vastness of God and the limitations of our finite minds in fully comprehending its true nature, fostering a sense of reverence and humility.

This line also reminds us to approach the sacred with humility and respect. It calls upon us to purify our thoughts, words, and actions, aligning ourselves with the highest ideals of love, compassion, and truth. In doing so, we honor the holiness within our own beings, reflecting God spark that animates all life.

"THY KINGDOM COME, THY WILL BE DONE": SURRENDERING TO GOD'S DIVINE PLAN.

As we progress through the prayer, we encounter the powerful phrase, *"Thy kingdom come, thy will be done." This* line invites us to surrender our limited perspectives and embrace the vast, cosmic plan that unfolds according to God will.

The concept of *"Thy kingdom"* speaks to the ultimate sovereignty of God, reminding us that a higher order exists and a greater purpose beyond our immediate comprehension. It calls upon us to transcend the confines of our desires and align ourselves with the grand tapestry of creation, placing our trust in the wisdom that guides the universe's unfolding.

The phrase *"thy will be done"* is a profound surrender, a recognition that true peace and fulfillment arise from aligning our lives with the sacred flow of existence. It invites us to let go of our attachments and resistance, embracing the present moment with an open heart and a willingness to embrace life's lessons and challenges.

By surrendering to God's will, we open ourselves to boundless possibilities beyond our limited perspectives, allowing the sacred to guide our steps and reveal the deeper meaning and purpose that permeate our existence.

"GIVE US THIS DAY OUR DAILY BREAD": TRUSTING GOD'S PROVISION.

The Lord's Prayer reminds us of the fundamental need for sustenance and nourishment. The phrase "Give us this day our daily bread" is a humble request for the provisions necessary to sustain our physical and spiritual lives.

On a physical level, this line acknowledges our dependence on the earth's bounty and the cycle of life that provides for our material needs. It recognizes that true abundance flows from a deep connection with God and trusts that our basic needs will be met through the grace of the Creator.

Yet, this line also carries a spiritual significance. "Bread" can be interpreted as a metaphor for the nourishment that sustains our souls, the wisdom and guidance that feed our spiritual hunger. By asking for our "daily bread," we acknowledge our need for constant renewal and sustenance, recognizing that true fulfillment arises from a continuous connection with the sacred source.

This line invites us to cultivate a sense of trust and gratitude, embracing the present moment and the abundance surrounding us while simultaneously seeking the spiritual nourishment that sustains our journey toward wholeness and enlightenment.

"Forgive us our trespasses, as we forgive those who trespass against us": Embracing forgiveness and reconciliation.

During our spiritual journey, we inevitably encounter challenges, missteps, and moments of discord. The Lord's Prayer acknowledges this reality and offers a profound path toward healing and reconciliation through the phrase, *"Forgive us our trespasses, as we forgive those who trespass against us."*

This line recognizes our imperfections and the inherent flaws that can lead us astray. It is a humble acknowledgment of our shortcomings and a plea for divine forgiveness, rooted in the understanding that true growth and transformation arise from a willingness to confront our mistakes and seek redemption.

Yet, this line also powerfully calls us to extend the same forgiveness to others we seek. By forgiving those who have wronged us, we release the burdens of resentment and bitterness, opening our hearts to the healing power of compassion and understanding.

This act of forgiveness is not merely a superficial gesture but a profound recognition of our interconnectedness. It reminds us that just as we seek forgiveness for our transgressions, we must be willing to offer the same grace to others, fostering a spirit of reconciliation and unity that transcends the boundaries of individual suffering.

"Lead us not into temptation, but deliver us from evil": Seeking God's guidance and protection.

As we navigate the complexities of our spiritual journey, we are inevitably faced with temptations and challenges that can lead us astray. The Lord's Prayer acknowledges this reality and offers a powerful plea for divine guidance and protection: *"Lead us not into temptation, but deliver us from evil."*

This line recognizes the presence of forces that can distract us from our spiritual path, whether they manifest as internal struggles or external influences. It is a humble acknowledgment of our vulnerability and a recognition that we cannot overcome these challenges through sheer willpower alone.

When we seek God's guidance, He illuminates our path and gives us the wisdom to navigate life's complex challenges with a clear sense of purpose. This assures us that we are not alone, as God is omnipresent and always there to offer guidance and protect us when we accept His loving embrace. *" Hebrews say, "Jesus Christ is the same yesterday and today and forever. "* He never changes; he remains the same even throughout eternity.

Furthermore, "deliver us from evil" extends beyond physical or material adversities. It speaks to the need for deliverance from the darker aspects of our nature—the ego, fear, and negativity that can cloud our judgment and lead us astray. By seeking this deliverance, we open ourselves to the transformative power of the sacred, which has the potential to profoundly change us, purify our hearts and minds, and align us with the Father.

While the Lord's Prayer is often recited as a sacred ritual, its true power lies in our ability to embody its teachings and integrate them into our daily lives. By doing so, we can unlock the transformative potential of this powerful invocation and deepen our relationship with God.

1. **Cultivate Reverence and Humility**: The opening lines of the prayer remind us to approach God with a sense of awe and Reverence, acknowledging our limitations. In our daily lives, we can cultivate this Reverence by embracing a spirit of wonder and gratitude, appreciating the intricate beauty and the complexity of the world around us.
2. **Surrender to God Plan**: The call to surrender to God's will invites us to let go of our need for control and embrace the unfolding of life with trust and acceptance. In our daily lives, we can practice this surrender by embracing the present

moment, releasing our attachments, and allowing God to guide our steps.

3. **Embrace Forgiveness and Reconciliation**: The powerful message of forgiveness and reconciliation reminds us of the healing power of compassion and understanding. In our daily interactions, we can strive to embody these principles by letting go of resentments, seeking to understand others' perspectives, and fostering a spirit of unity and harmony.

4. **Seek Guidance and Protection:** The plea for God's guidance and protection reminds us that we are not alone in our journey and that the sacred is ever-present to support and guide us. We can cultivate this connection in our daily lives by practicing mindfulness, seeking wisdom, and remaining open to God's will.

5. **Cultivate Gratitude and Trust**: The request for daily provisions reminds us to embrace a spirit of gratitude and trust in the universe's abundance. We can cultivate this attitude daily by appreciating our blessings, focusing on what we have rather than what we lack, and trusting that our needs will be met.

Integrating these lessons into our daily lives allows us to transform the Lord's Prayer from a mere recitation into a living, breathing practice that guides our thoughts, words, and actions. In doing so, we deepen our connection with the sacred and align ourselves with the highest expression of our true selves.

The Lord's Prayer is timeless and has guided countless souls on their spiritual journeys. By unveiling the meaning embedded within each line, we uncover the depths of wisdom that strengthen our relationship with God. The Lord's Prayer offers a roadmap for our spiritual growth and teaches us to surrender and trust the Lord. We must learn to embrace forgiveness and reconciliation and seek guidance and protection.

As we learn the lessons of the Lord's Prayer, we open ourselves to boundless possibilities. We cultivate a deeper connection with God and align ourselves with the highest expression of love, compassion, and truth. Reciting the Lord's Prayer is not a mere ritual but a dynamic and life-changing habit that permeates our innermost beings. It gives us a golden opportunity to draw closer to the Lord and experience joy even during spiritual darkness.

Chapter 9
Praying the Psalms

The Book of Psalms, a timeless treasure trove of divinely inspired prayers and praises, has been a source of solace and strength for countless souls throughout the ages. This sacred text, penned by various authors under the guidance of the Holy Spirit, offers a connection with God, allowing us to pour out our hearts and find refuge in the embrace of our Heavenly Father.

As we venture deeper into the Psalms, an exquisite image of human sentiment unfolds before us—a tapestry interwoven with shades of elation, anguish, expectancy, and trepidation, all bound together in a beautiful symphony of words.

Through the Psalms, we are invited to join the psalmists in praise, lament, and supplication, experiencing the transformative power of prayer that has sustained generations of believers. Whether we seek comfort in times of crisis, guidance in moments of uncertainty, or a deeper intimacy with God.

THE POWER OF PRAYING THE PSALMS

Praying the Psalms is a transformative practice that can shape our souls and deepen our relationship with God. We access spiritual wisdom and strength when we speak these inspired words.

The Psalms are not mere poetic verses; they are living prayers that carry the weight of eternity. As we pray to them, we become part of an unbroken chain of faith, joining our voices with those of the psalmists and countless generations of believers who have found solace and strength in these sacred words.

Furthermore, the Psalms resonate uniquely with the depths of our souls, giving voice to the emotions and experiences that often elude our own words. Whether rejoicing in the Lord's goodness or lamenting amid trials, the Psalms provide a language that transcends our limited understanding, allowing us to pour out our hearts before the Throne of Grace.

By praying the Psalms, we express our deepest longings and praises and invite the transformative power of God's Word to shape our thoughts, emotions, and actions. As we meditate on these ancient prayers, we gradually conform to the image of Christ, our minds renewed, and our hearts aligned with the heart of our Heavenly Father.

UNDERSTANDING THE STRUCTURE OF THE PSALMS

1. Understanding the unique structure and composition of the Book of Psalms is essential to fully appreciate the power of praying when using them during prayer. The Book is divided into five sections, each with its theme and purpose.

2. **Book I (Psalms 1-41):** This section focuses on the blessings of righteousness and the consequences of wickedness, emphasizing the importance of trusting God and obeying His commands.

3. **Book II (Psalms 42-72):** The Psalms explore the themes of suffering, deliverance, and God's sovereignty, providing comfort and hope in times of distress.

4. **Book III (Psalms 73-89):** This section delves into the complexities of life, addressing questions of justice, the

prosperity of the wicked, and God's enduring faithfulness.
5. **Book IV (Psalms 90-106)**: These Psalms celebrate God's majesty and power, inviting us to worship Him and trust in His steadfast love.
6. **Book V (Psalms 107-150)**: The final section is a collection of praise and thanksgiving, culminating in a grand crescendo of worship and adoration of the Almighty.

Understanding the structure of the Psalms is crucial to fully appreciating their depth and richness. This knowledge enables us to engage with these holy prayers more deeply and meaningfully.

BENEFITS OF PRAYING THE BOOK OF PSALMS

Praying the Book of Psalms is a transformative practice that yields numerous spiritual benefits. Here are some of the profound ways in which the Psalms can enrich our lives and deepen our relationship with God:

1. **Emotional Healing**: The Psalms provide a safe haven to express our deepest emotions, whether joy, sorrow, anger, or

fear. We find comfort and healing as we pray these words, knowing that the God who created us understands and validates our feelings.

2. **Spiritual Nourishment**: The Psalms are a rich source of spiritual sustenance, offering wisdom, guidance, and encouragement for our souls. As we meditate on these prayers, we are nourished by the very Word of God, strengthening our faith, and deepening our trust in the Almighty.

3. **Intimacy with God**: Praying the Psalms is an intimate conversation with our Heavenly Father. We pour out our hearts, share our struggles, and express our praises, fostering a closer relationship with the One who knows us better than we know ourselves.

4. **Perspective and Wisdom**: The Psalms provide a divine perspective on life's challenges and complexities, offering wisdom and insight that transcend our limited understanding. As we pray these words, our minds are renewed, and our outlook is transformed, enabling us to

navigate life's difficulties with grace and faith.
5. **Worship and Praise**: The Psalms are a powerful tool for prayer and praise, allowing us to express our adoration and gratitude to the Almighty profoundly and meaningfully. As we pray these words, our hearts are lifted, and our spirits are renewed, reminding us of the greatness and majesty of our God.

HOW TO START PRAYING THE PSALMS

If you are new to praying the Psalms, fear not – the journey begins with a single step. Here are some practical tips to help you embark on this transformative spiritual **practice:**

1. **Start Small:** Select a few Psalms that resonate with your current circumstances or emotions. Slowly incorporate them into your daily prayer routine, allowing the words to sink into your heart and mind.
2. **Choose a Translation:** Decide on a Bible translation that speaks to you personally. Some prefer the poetic language of the

King James Version, while others find modern translations more accessible.
3. **Set Aside Time:** Dedicate a specific time each day for praying the Psalms. This sacred ritual will help you establish a consistent habit and create a space for undistracted communion with God.
4. **Personalize the Prayers:** As you pray the Psalms, make them your own. Substitute personal pronouns and situations, allowing the words to become a genuine expression of your heart's desires and struggles.
5. **Reflect and Meditate:** After praying a Psalm, take a moment to reflect on the words and their meaning. Allow the Holy Spirit to illuminate your understanding and reveal the depths of God's truth and love.

Remember, praying the Psalms is a journey, and developing a rhythm and familiarity with these sacred prayers may take time. Be patient with yourself, and trust that the Lord will meet you in these moments of intimate communion.

DIFFERENT WAYS TO PRAY THE PSALMS

While praying the Psalms is a profound spiritual practice, there are various approaches you can explore to enrich your experience and deepen your connection with God's Word. Here are some different ways to pray the Psalms:

1. **Responsive Reading:** This method involves reading the Psalms aloud, individually or with a group, alternating between verses or sections. This practice allows the words to resonate within you and creates a sense of unity and community.
2. **Lectio Divina:** Lectio Divina, or "divine reading," is an ancient practice of meditating on Scripture. It involves four steps: reading, meditation, prayer, and contemplation. This approach encourages you to slow down, savor the words, and allow the Holy Spirit to speak to your heart.
3. **Psalm Journaling:** As you pray the Psalms, consider keeping a journal to record your thoughts, reflections, and personal experiences. This practice not only aids in

memorization but also provides a tangible record of your spiritual journey.
4. **Psalm Memorization:** Committing Psalms to memory is a powerful way to carry God's Word with you throughout the day. Memorized verses can provide comfort, encouragement, and strength in need.
5. **Psalm Singing or Chanting:** Many Psalms were initially composed as songs or chants. Exploring this musical aspect can add depth and richness to your prayer experience, allowing the words to resonate uniquely and powerfully within your soul.
6. **Psalm Visualization:** As you pray the Psalms, visualize the scenes and imagery described in the verses. This practice can help you connect with the Scriptures deeper, bringing the words to life and making them more tangible.

Remember, there is no one-size-fits-all approach to praying the Psalms. Experiment with different methods and find the most resonating with your personal style and spiritual needs. The beauty of the Psalms lies in their ability to speak to everyone uniquely and profoundly.

EXAMPLES OF PSALMS FOR SPECIFIC SITUATIONS
The Book of Psalms is a rich tapestry of prayers covering various human experiences and emotions. Here are some examples of Psalms that can provide comfort, guidance, and strength in specific situations:

1. **In Times of Distress** and Anxiety, Psalms 23, 27, 46, and 91 offer reassurance and peace, reminding us of God's unwavering presence and protection.
2. **When Seeking Forgiveness:** Psalms 32, 51, and 130 are potent prayers of repentance, expressing heartfelt sorrow and a longing for God's mercy and restoration.
3. **During Seasons of Praise and Thanksgiving,** Psalms 100, 103, and 145 are joyful expressions of gratitude and adoration, inviting us to celebrate God's goodness and faithfulness.
4. **In Moments of Despair and Lament,** Psalms 13, 22, and 88 voice our deepest sorrows and struggles, reminding us that

even in our darkest moments, God hears our cries and understands our pain.
5. **When Seeking Wisdom and Guidance:** Psalms 1, 19, and 119 offer insights and instruction, guiding us in righteousness and helping us navigate life's complexities.
6. **Times of Persecution or Oppression,** Psalms 7, 35, and 109 comfort and strengthen those facing injustice or oppression, reminding us that God is our refuge and defender.
7. **For Spiritual Renewal and Restoration:** Psalms 42, 63, and 84 express a deep longing for intimacy with God and a desire for spiritual refreshment, inviting us to find our strength and joy in the Presence of the Almighty.

These examples are merely a starting point, as the Psalms offer a wealth of prayers and praises for every circumstance and season of life. As you explore the Book of Psalms, allow the Holy Spirit to guide you to the specific verses that speak to your unique situation and needs.

As we end our exploration of the power of praying the Book of Psalms, we are reminded of their timeless relevance and profound impact. The Psalms are a gift from God, a treasure trove of wisdom, comfort, and strength that has sustained generations of believers throughout the ages.

Embracing praying the Psalms is a spiritual exercise and a journey of intimacy with our Heavenly Father. As we utter these divinely inspired words, we join our voices with the psalmists of old, becoming part of an unbroken chain of faith that spans centuries and transcends cultures.

The Psalms can heal our wounds, renew our minds, and transform our lives. They provide a haven for us to express our deepest emotions, a sanctuary where we can find solace and refuge in the embrace of our loving God. The Psalms remind us that our struggles, fears, and joys are understood and validated by the One who created and knows us intimately.

As we continue to pray the Psalms, may we be filled with a renewed sense of awe and wonder at the majesty and love of our God. May these ancient prayers become a wellspring of hope, a source of strength, and a constant reminder of the unwavering presence of the Almighty in our lives.

So, let us embrace the power of the Book of Psalms, allowing these sacred words to shape our hearts, guide our steps, and deepen our relationship with the One who is the author and perfecter of our faith.

If the power of the Psalms has touched you and you desire to deepen your prayer life, we invite you to join our online community dedicated to exploring the richness of these sacred prayers. Through our weekly virtual gatherings, you can pray the Psalms together, share your experiences, and receive guidance and support on your spiritual journey. Join us today and experience the transformative power of the Book of Psalms in a community of like-minded believers. Visit

Chapter 10
Standing Firm on God's Promises

As we navigate life's intricate paths, anchoring ourselves in God's promises is essential. These promises serve as a beacon of hope and strength, guiding us through the challenges and uncertainties that lie ahead.

God's promises are more than words; they are His assurances that we are not alone. They are the promises woven throughout the pages of Scripture, revealing the depth of God's love, faithfulness, and commitment to His children. They are not empty utterances but solemn vows that have withstood the test of time, transcending generations, and cultures.

Standing firm on God's promises is foundational to our Christian faith. It declares our trust in the One who cannot lie and whose word is eternal. When we cling to these promises, we acknowledge that our lives are not governed by chance or circumstance but by the sovereign hand of the Almighty. This unwavering stance fortifies our faith, empowering us to face adversity with courage and resilience.

EXAMPLES OF GOD'S PROMISES IN THE BIBLE
The Bible is a treasure trove of God's promises, each a testament to His faithfulness and love. Consider these robust assurances:

1. **Provision**: "And my God will meet all your needs according to the riches of his glory in Christ Jesus." (Philippians 4:19)
2. **Protection**: "The Lord is my rock, my fortress and my deliverer; my God is my rock, in whom I take refuge, my shield and the horn of my salvation, my stronghold." (Psalm 18:2)
3. **Guidance**: "Trust in the Lord with all your heart and lean not on your own understanding; in all your ways submit to him, and he will make your paths straight." (Proverbs 3:5-6)

These are a few examples of the countless promises our Heavenly Father has bestowed upon us, reminding us of His unwavering love and care.

HOW TO HOLD ONTO GOD'S PROMISES DURING CHALLENGING TIMES

Holding onto God's promises during challenging times is a testament to our faith and trust in Him. When the storms of life rage, it can be tempting to allow doubt and fear to creep in. However, we must cling to His promises with even more extraordinary tenacity during these moments.

One practical way to hold onto God's promises is to write them down and keep them close at hand. Seeing the written word can be a powerful reminder of God's faithfulness, providing comfort and strength when we need it most.

Another practical approach is to meditate on God's promises, allowing them to sink deep into our hearts and minds. Through prayerful reflection, we can better understand their significance and apply them to our circumstances.

TRUSTING IN GOD'S TIMING AND FAITHFULNESS

Trusting in God's promises and perfect timing is crucial. Embracing His plans demands patience and persistence, but we can find solace in knowing that He is tirelessly working behind the scenes, orchestrating events for our ultimate benefit, and glorifying His name.

SEEKING GUIDANCE AND STRENGTH THROUGH PRAYER AND MEDITATION

Prayer and meditation are crucial to keeping God's promises. We can seek His guidance, wisdom, and strength through earnest communication with our Heavenly Father. Prayer allows us to pour out our hearts, express our concerns, and find solace in His presence.

Meditation, on the other hand, is the practice of quieting our minds and hearts, creating space to listen to the gentle whispers of the Holy Spirit. As we meditate on God's Word and His promises, we open ourselves to receiving divine revelation and insights that can profoundly transform our lives, filling us with inspiration and hope.

A SUPPORTIVE COMMUNITY OF BELIEVERS

The journey of standing firm on God's promises is not one we must undertake alone. God has designed us to be part of a community of believers, a spiritual family that can uplift, encourage, and support one another. Surrounding ourselves with like-minded individuals who share our commitment to God's promises can provide invaluable encouragement and accountability.

Through fellowship, Bible studies, and shared experiences, we can learn from one another's testimonies, gain wisdom from those who have walked the path before us, and find strength in the unity of our faith. These shared experiences connect us and provide a strong support system in our spiritual journey.

In conclusion, we steadfastly hold onto God's promises and fully embrace the life-changing truth they bring. Let us always remember that our Heavenly Father is faithful and trustworthy in fulfilling His pledges to us. By grounding ourselves in His teachings and relying on His unwavering assurances, we welcome a profound encounter with his boundless love, provision, and guidance for all eternity.

Chapter 11

Unlocking the Power of Intercessory Prayer

As believers, we are called to a life of prayer, not just for ourselves but also for others. Intercessory prayer, the act of praying on behalf of someone else, is a powerful tool God gives us. It is a privilege and a responsibility that allows us to partner with God in transforming the lives of those we lift up in prayer.

Intercessory prayer enables us to serve as vessels for God's grace, mercy, and love. We advocate for others, praying on their behalf and seeking God's intervention. Whether longing for physical healing, emotional restoration, or spiritual renewal for those around us, our intercessory prayers can touch God's heart and unleash His blessings upon those we lift up. Intercessory prayer is more than just speaking to God—it is a sacred conversation with the Almighty. By interceding for others, we invite the

Holy Spirit to guide our prayers and align our requests with God's divine purpose.

THE POWER OF INTERCESSORY PRAYER

The power of intercessory prayer lies in its ability to transcend time and space, reaching into the lives of those we pray for, regardless of their physical location or circumstances. Through our prayers, we invite the presence of God into their situations, and His power is unleashed to work in ways that we cannot fully comprehend.

Intercessory prayer is not limited by our understanding or ability to articulate our requests perfectly. The Holy Spirit intercedes for us with "groanings too deep for words" (Romans 8:26), ensuring that our Heavenly Father hears and understands our prayers.

Moreover, intercessory prayer can influence the spiritual realm, engaging in spiritual warfare against the forces of darkness that seek to undermine God's purposes. As we pray, we align ourselves with God's will and actively participate in His redemptive work.

BIBLICAL EXAMPLES OF INTERCESSORY PRAYER

The Bible is replete with examples of individuals who interceded on behalf of others, and their prayers brought about changes. Consider the prophet Samuel, who interceded for the Israelites, and God responded by sending thunder and rain during the wheat harvest (1 Samuel 12:16-18). The apostle Paul consistently prayed for his established churches, seeking their spiritual growth and protection (Ephesians 1:15-23, Philippians 1:9-11).

One of the most potent examples is that of Jesus Himself, who interceded for His disciples and all believers (John 17:1-26). His high priestly prayer is a model for us, demonstrating the depth of love and concern we should have for those we pray for.

How to pray effectively as an intercessor

Effective intercessory prayer requires a heart aligned with God's will and a mind focused on His purposes. As intercessors, we must cultivate a lifestyle of worship, seeking the Lord's guidance and direction for our prayers.

One key aspect of effective intercessory prayer is persistence. We are called to pray without ceasing (1 Thessalonians 5:17), trusting that God hears our petitions and will answer in His perfect timing. Additionally, we must pray with faith, believing God can do more than we can ask or imagine (Ephesians 3:20).

It is also essential to pray humbly, recognizing that we are vessels through which God's power flows. We must surrender our desires and agendas, seeking only to align ourselves with God's will for the lives of those we pray for.

Intercessory prayer is not just a spiritual exercise; it can bring about tangible transformation in our personal lives, communities, and even nations. As we pray for others, we open ourselves to the work of the Holy Spirit, who refines and shapes us into the image of Christ.

Moreover, intercessory prayer can shift the spiritual climate of our communities. When we unite in prayer, we create a spiritual atmosphere conducive to God's move. Our prayers can break down strongholds, open doors for the gospel, and prepare the way for revival and spiritual awakening.

Intercessory prayer also plays a vital role in advancing God's kingdom on earth. As we pray for the lost, for the persecuted church, and for the spread of the gospel, we participate in the great commission and become co-laborers with Christ in the work of redemption.

INTERCESSORY PRAYER AND SPIRITUAL WARFARE

Intercessory prayer is both a passive activity and an active engagement in spiritual warfare. The apostle Paul reminds us that our struggle is not against flesh and blood but against the rulers, authorities, and cosmic powers of this present darkness (Ephesians 6:12). As we pray for others, we confront the forces of evil that seek to enslave and oppress them.

Through intercessory prayer, we can bind the enemy's work and lose God's power in the lives of those we pray for. We can tear down spiritual strongholds, break generational curses, and declare Christ's victory over the powers of darkness.

However, it is essential to remember that our battle is not against people but against the spiritual forces that influence and deceive them. Our prayers should be rooted in love, compassion, and a desire to see people set free from the bondage of sin and darkness.

STORIES OF DIVINE INTERVENTION

Throughout history, there have been countless stories of divine intervention and miraculous answers to prayer due to intercessory prayer. These stories serve as a testament to the power of prayer and encourage us to persevere in our prayer lives.

One powerful example is the story of the Welsh Revival in 1904-1905. It began with a group of young people who committed to fervent prayer, seeking a spiritual awakening in their community. Their prayers were answered powerfully, and a revival swept through Wales, leading to thousands of conversions and a profound impact on the nation.

Another inspiring story is that of Rees Howells, a Welsh intercessor who played a pivotal role in the spiritual battles of World War II. Through his unwavering commitment to intercessory prayer, he and his prayer partners saw remarkable answers to prayer, including preserving lives and turning crucial battles.

These stories remind us that our prayers can shape history and impact the course of nations. They encourage us to persevere in prayer, trusting that God hears and answers the cries of His people.

Intercessory prayer is a sacred privilege and a powerful tool that God has given us to partner with Him in advancing His kingdom and transforming the lives of others. As we commit ourselves to praying for others, we unlock the power of heaven and become vessels through which God's grace and mercy flow.

Remember, intercessory prayer is not just a spiritual exercise; it is a lifestyle of standing in the gap for others, interceding on their behalf, and petitioning the throne of grace for their needs. The journey requires perseverance, faith, and a heart aligned with God's will.

Chapter 12

Embracing the Role of a Prayer Warrior

As believers, we are called to be prayer warriors, spiritual soldiers engaged in a constant battle against the forces of darkness. We recognize the power of prayer, a potent weapon in the spiritual realm, and use it to advance God's kingdom. We are not merely passive observers but active participants.

The role of a prayer warrior is multifaceted. We are intercessors, standing in the gap for others and lifting their needs before the throne of grace. We are petitioners, presenting our requests to our Heavenly Father with unwavering faith. We are worshippers, exalting the name of the Lord and seeking His face in adoration.

Moreover, we are warriors, clad in the whole armor of God, ready to confront the schemes of the enemy. Our prayers are not mere words but powerful declarations that shake the foundations of the spiritual realm. As prayer warriors, we are called to be vigilant, persistent, and unyielding in our pursuit of God's purposes.

THE POWER OF PRAYER IN SPIRITUAL WARFARE

Prayer isn't just a routine. It is a powerful force that can shape events in the lives of those who believe in God's power. The Bible contains examples of individuals whose prayers moved God's hand and brought about remarkable transformations.

When we pray, we communicate directly with God. Our prayers can change atmospheres, break strongholds, and bring about divine intervention. This connection aligns us with God's will and the limitless resources of Heaven.

HOW TO BECOME A PRAYER WARRIOR

Becoming a prayer warrior is not a mere title; it is a lifestyle, a journey of surrender and intimacy with God. Here are some steps to help you embrace this calling:

1. **Cultivate a personal relationship with God**: Prayer is not a one-way monologue but a dialogue with our Heavenly Father. It involves spending time in His presence,

reading His Word, and nurturing a deep connection with Him.
2. **Develop a prayer strategy**: Identify specific areas or individuals for whom you will intercede. Create a prayer journal or list to help you stay focused and organized in your prayer life.
3. **Join a prayer community**: Surround yourself with like-minded believers who share your passion for prayer. Participate in corporate prayer meetings to experience the power of united prayer.
4. **Persevere in prayer**: Prayer is not a one-time event but a continuous journey. Commit to praying without ceasing, even when circumstances seem unchanging. Remember, God's timing is perfect, and He is faithful in answering our prayers according to His will.

DEVELOPING A STRONG PRAYER LIFE

Cultivating a solid prayer life is essential for anyone aspiring to be a prayer warrior. Here are some practical tips to help you strengthen your prayer life:

1. **Set aside dedicated prayer times**: Establish a consistent routine for prayer, whether it's in the morning, evening, or throughout the day. Treat these times as sacred appointments with God.
2. **Create a prayer space**: Designate a quiet place in your home or workplace where you can pray without distractions. This space can help you focus and create an atmosphere conducive to prayer.
3. **Incorporate various prayer methods**: Explore different practices, such as praise and worship, intercessory prayer, prayer walks, or fasting and prayer. Variety can keep your prayer life fresh and engaging.
4. **Study the Scriptures**: Ground your prayers in the Word of God. Allow the Scriptures to shape your prayers and deepen your understanding of God's character and promises.
5. **Keep a prayer journal**: Record your prayer requests, answered prayers, and spiritual insights. Journaling can help you track God's faithfulness and encourage your faith.

PRAYING WITH PURPOSE AND INTENTION

As prayer warriors, it is essential to pray with purpose and intention. Our prayers should be focused, specific, and aligned with the will of God. Here are some guidelines to help you pray with intention:

1. **Pray according to God's will**: Study the Scriptures to understand God's heart and desires. Align your prayers with His revealed will and purposes.
2. **Pray with faith**: Approach the throne of grace with unwavering faith, believing that God can do abundantly beyond all we ask or think (Ephesians 3:20).
3. **Pray with persistence**: Stay energized and energized in your prayers. Keep knocking, keep seeking, and keep asking until you receive an answer from the Lord (Luke 11:9-10).
4. **Pray with authority**: As believers, we have been given authority in Jesus' name. Pray confidently, rebuking the works of darkness and commanding breakthroughs in the spiritual realm.

5. **Pray with discernment**: Seek the guidance of the Holy Spirit as you pray. Ask for wisdom and discernment to pray according to God's perfect will and timing.

As we embrace our role as prayer warriors, we position ourselves to experience the fullness of God's power and witness His miraculous works unfold. Prayer is not merely a spiritual discipline but a potent weapon that can transform lives, nations, and the course of history.

When we pray with enthusiasm, faith, and persistence, we unleash the power of Heaven upon the earth. Our prayers can break chains, heal the sick, and usher in revival. As prayer warriors, we are called to stand firm in the face of opposition, never wavering in our commitment to intercession.

Remember, our battles are not against flesh and blood but against principalities and powers in the spiritual realm (Ephesians 6:12). Therefore, let us clothe ourselves with the whole armor of God and engage in spiritual warfare through prayer.

Experience the power of prayer and embrace your role as a prayer warrior. Together, we can unleash God's power and witness His transformative work in our lives, families, and communities.

May we never underestimate the power of prayer or the significance of our role as prayer warriors. Let us boldly approach the throne of grace, confident in the knowledge that our prayers are heard and that our Heavenly Father delights in answering the earnest petitions of His children.

Chapter 13
Recognizing God's Answer to Prayer

Recognizing God's voice can sometimes be difficult, given our busy lives. God often responds to our prayers in subtle ways. It might be a quiet voice in our thoughts, a sudden realization, or reflecting on past events that shows God's guiding hand. When we surrender our fears, doubts, and desires to the foot of the cross, we open ourselves to receiving the wisdom, guidance, and solace we desperately seek.

As we continue to pray and seek guidance, our capacity to receive and interpret God's revelations grows stronger. We begin recognizing the patterns and signs guiding us toward our answer. Divine revelations can manifest in myriad forms, each tailored to our unique spiritual journey and personal meaning. It is important to approach these revelations with an open mind and a discerning heart, for the language of God is often subtle and deeply personal.

1. **Intuitive Nudges**: These gentle whispers arise from within, guiding us towards certain decisions or actions. They may come as a sudden clarity, a solid inner knowing, or a persistent feeling that cannot be ignored. Trusting these intuitive nudges is a powerful act of faith, as they often defy logic and rational thinking.
2. **Synchronicities**: These are meaningful coincidences that occur in our lives, seemingly orchestrated by God. They may manifest as repeated number sequences, symbolic encounters, or serendipitous events that defy the laws of probability. Recognizing these expressions is divine communication.
3. **Dreams and Visions**: Throughout biblical history, God communicated with His people through signs, visions, and dreams. Dreams often reveal what is locked away in our hearts and minds. There, we may find the answer we are looking for: God's answer.
4. **Scriptures**: Answers to our prayers are often discovered in Scripture. Consistent study of God's word can help reveal

solutions to unanswered questions and provide guidance and wisdom. Jay Adams, a well-known Nouthetic author, believed that most answers to life's questions can be found in the Scriptures. Sometimes, the answers we seek are right there in the pages of the Bible.

HOW TO RECOGNIZE AND INTERPRET DIVINE RESPONSES

When seeking to hear from God, it is essential to exercise spiritual discernment. Spiritual discernment involves distinguishing between God's voice and other influences, such as distractions or the deceptive tactics of the adversary. It is essential to be vigilant and attentive to genuinely tune in to God's voice amidst the noise and confusion that may surround us.

1. **Cultivate Stillness**: In the fast-paced modern world, it is easy to lose touch with God's guidance and purpose. Creating moments of stillness allows us to open ourselves to God's teachings and wisdom.

2. **Trust Your Intuition**: Divine revelations often come in intuitive nudges or gut feelings. Learn to trust these inner promptings, even when they defy logic or rational thinking. Our intuition is a powerful tool that can guide us toward divine alignment.
3. **Observe Synchronicities**: Pay attention to meaningful coincidences in your life. These synchronicities can be powerful indicators of divine guidance, revealing hidden connections and messages tailored specifically to you.
4. **Seek Guidance and Wisdom**: While divine revelations are deeply personal, seeking guidance from spiritual teachers, elders, or trusted mentors can provide valuable insights and perspectives. Their wisdom and experience can help you navigate the complexities of interpreting God's messages.
5. **Maintain an Open Mind**: Approach God's revelations with a curious mindset. God's message can be subtle and unconventional, challenging our preconceived notions and beliefs.

Embrace the mystery and allow yourself to be guided by the wisdom that unfolds before you.

Always remember that interpreting God's revelations is a continuous journey of spiritual growth. It requires patience, humility, and a willingness to surrender to God's plan for your life. Trust that the guidance you seek will unfold in God's perfect timing.

STEPS TO ENHANCE YOUR ABILITY TO RECEIVE DIVINE REVELATIONS

While divine revelations are ultimately a gift from God, specific practices and mindsets can enhance our ability to receive and interpret these sacred messages. By cultivating a receptive state of being, we open ourselves to the infinite wisdom and guidance the Universe offers.

1. **Cultivate a Mindset of Gratitude**: Approach each day with a heart overflowing with gratitude. Express appreciation for the blessings in your life, both big and small. This mindset of appreciation creates a vibration that

resonates with God, opening channels for divine revelations to flow more freely.

2. **Practice Mindfulness and Presence**: By anchoring ourselves in the present moment, we become more attuned to subtle whispers and nudges from within. Mindfulness practices such as meditation, deep breathing, or being present during everyday tasks can cultivate this heightened awareness.

3. **Embrace Surrender and Trust**: Letting go of our need for control and surrendering to God's plan is a powerful act of faith. By trusting that the Universe has an excellent plan for us, we open ourselves to receive the guidance and revelations that align with our highest good.

4. **Seek Solitude and Silence**: Stillness and solitude create a sacred space for divine revelations. Set aside dedicated time for prayer, meditation, or simply being in nature, allowing the world's noise to fade away and the whispers of God to emerge.

5. **Cultivate a Beginner's Mind**: Approach each experience with curiosity and openness, free from preconceived notions

or judgments. This beginner's mind allows us to perceive the world with fresh eyes, unveiling hidden messages and revelations that our limited perspectives may have obscured.

6. **Seek Guidance from Spiritual Mentors**: While receiving divine revelations is deeply personal, seeking guidance from spiritual mentors, teachers, or elders can provide invaluable insights and support. Their wisdom and experience can help us navigate the complexities of this sacred path.

7. **Practice Self-Reflection and Journaling**: Regularly reflecting on your experiences and documenting your insights through journaling can help you identify patterns, synchronicities, and divine messages that may have initially gone unnoticed. This practice also cultivates a deeper self-awareness and connection to your inner guidance.

Remember, enhancing your ability to receive divine revelations is a continuous journey of self-discovery and spiritual growth. Approach each step with patience, dedication, and an open heart, trusting that God will reveal its wisdom in perfect timing and in a manner that resonates with your unique soul's journey.

COMMON MISCONCEPTIONS ABOUT DIVINE REVELATIONS

As we delve into the realm of divine revelations, it is essential to address and dispel some common misconceptions that may arise. By clarifying these misunderstandings, we can approach this sacred journey with greater clarity and a deeper understanding of God's wisdom that awaits us.

1. **Divine Revelations are Exclusive to Spiritual Leaders or Mystics**: One of the most prevalent misconceptions is that divine revelations are reserved for a select few, such as spiritual leaders, mystics, or those who have attained a certain level of enlightenment. However, the truth is that divine revelations are available to all who are open and receptive to receiving them. God does not discriminate; it speaks to each soul in a language that resonates with their unique journey.

2. **Divine Revelations Are Always Grandiose or Earth-Shattering**: Many believe that divine revelations must be profound, life-altering experiences that shake the very foundations of our existence. While such profound revelations do occur, the reality is that divine guidance often manifests in subtle, seemingly mundane ways. It may come as a gentle nudge, a synchronistic event, or a simple sign that holds profound significance for our personal journey.
3. **Divine Revelations Require Specific Rituals or Practices**: While certain spiritual practices and rituals can enhance our receptivity to divine revelations, the belief that specific methods are required can limit our understanding of God's infinite wisdom. The truth is that divine revelations can occur at any moment, during any activity, and in any setting as long as we remain open and attuned to the subtle whispers of the Universe.
4. **Divine Revelations Are Always Clear and Unambiguous**: Many assume that divine revelations should be crystal clear, leaving no room for interpretation or ambiguity.

However, the language of God is often symbolic, metaphorical, and deeply personal. Interpreting these revelations requires patience, discernment, and a willingness to explore the deeper layers of meaning that resonate with our unique experiences and spiritual journeys.

5. **Divine Revelations Provide Definitive Answers**: While divine revelations can offer guidance and insights, expecting them to provide definitive answers or solutions to life's challenges is a misconception. God often speaks in ways that encourage our personal growth, self-discovery, and spiritual evolution, inviting us to explore the depths of our own wisdom and inner knowing.

By dispelling these common misconceptions, we can approach the realm of divine revelations with an open mind and a deeper understanding of the infinite ways God communicates with us. Embracing the mystery and complexity of this sacred journey allows us to receive the wisdom and guidance tailored specifically for our unique souls.

PERSONAL TESTIMONIES OF DIVINE REVELATIONS

Throughout history, individuals from diverse backgrounds and spiritual traditions have shared powerful testimonies of divine revelations that have profoundly impacted their lives. These personal accounts serve as a reminder that God speaks to each soul in unique and profound ways, offering guidance, solace, and transformative insights.

1. **A Synchronistic Encounter**: "I had been struggling with a major life decision for months, feeling paralyzed by fear and uncertainty. One day, as I was walking through the park, a beautiful butterfly landed on my shoulder, and in that moment, I knew with absolute certainty that everything would unfold as it was meant to. The synchronicity of that encounter felt like a divine message, reminding me to trust the journey and let go of my need for control."
2. **A Vivid Dream**: "I had been grappling with a deep sense of grief and loss after the passing of a loved one. One night, I had a

vivid dream in which they appeared radiant and at peace. They conveyed a message of love and reassurance, reminding me that our connection transcends the physical realm. Upon waking, I felt a profound sense of healing and a renewed appreciation for life's and death's mysteries."

3. **A Sacred Symbol**: "During a particularly challenging period, I encountered the same symbol – a spiral – in various forms and contexts. Initially, I dismissed it as mere coincidence, but as the encounters became more frequent and significant, I felt compelled to explore its deeper meaning. Through research and self-reflection, I discovered that the spiral represented the cyclical nature of life, growth, and transformation. This divine revelation gave me the perspective and resilience to navigate my difficulties with grace and trust in the unfolding journey."

4. **An Intuitive Nudge**: "I had been considering a career change for some time, but fear and self-doubt kept holding me back. One day, while engaged in a routine

task, I felt an overwhelming sense of clarity and an unmistakable inner voice urging me to take the leap. It was as if the Universe was conspiring to nudge me toward my highest potential. I heeded the call, and that decision set me on a path of profound personal and professional fulfillment."

5. **A Serendipitous Encounter**: "During a particularly challenging time, I encountered a stranger who shared a profound insight tailored to my situation. It was as if the Universe had orchestrated our meeting, using this individual as a vessel to deliver a divine message of hope and guidance. The serendipity of the encounter left me in awe of the intricate ways in which God communicates with us."

These personal testimonies serve as a reminder that divine revelations can take many forms, from synchronistic events and vivid dreams to sacred symbols and intuitive nudges. They remind us that God speaks to each soul in a unique language, offering guidance, solace, and transformative insights that can profoundly impact our lives and our spiritual journeys.

As we conclude our exploration of divine revelations, it is evident that this sacred journey is one of profound depth, mystery, and personal transformation. Throughout this article, we have delved into the intricate ways God communicates with us, offering guidance, solace, and profound insights that can profoundly impact our lives and spiritual journeys.

We have learned that divine revelations can take many forms, from intuitive nudges and synchronistic events to vivid dreams and sacred symbols. Each revelation is tailored to our unique souls, speaking to us in a language that resonates with our personal experiences and spiritual resonance.

Recognizing and interpreting these divine messages requires a combination of attunement, discernment, and a willingness to trust the guidance that unfolds before us. By cultivating practices such as stillness, mindfulness, and surrender, we enhance our ability to receive and decode God's whispers.

Through personal testimonies, we have witnessed the profound impact that divine revelations can have. They offer solace, direction, and transformative insights that can reshape our perspectives and guide us toward our highest paths.

As we continue this sacred journey, we must remember that seeking guidance through prayer and meditation can deepen our connection with God and open channels for revelations to flow more freely. Additionally, exploring resources such as sacred texts, spiritual literature, workshops, and online communities can expand our understanding and provide valuable insights from those who have walked this path before us.

Ultimately, exploring divine revelations is a journey of self-discovery, faith, and surrender. It reminds us that we are never truly alone, for God is ever-present, guiding us with infinite wisdom and love. By embracing the mystery and complexity of this sacred exchange, we open ourselves to the profound transformations that await and to God's revelations that will illuminate our paths and enrich our souls.

Chapter 14
Unlocking the Power of the Prayer of Jabez

The Prayer of Jabez found in 1 Chronicles 4:9-10, is a powerful example of the transformative impact of faith and supplication. It has deeply inspired believers across generations, encouraging them to unlock their spiritual potential.

The Prayer of Jabez holds a unique place in biblical supplications. While its concise nature may belie its depth, this prayer encapsulates the essence of our relationship with God – founded on humility, trust, and an unwavering desire to walk in the light of divine favor.

These few verses provide a blueprint for a life lived in harmony with God's will. Jabez's prayer transcends the confines of time and space, resonating with the universal longing of the human spirit to find meaning, purpose, and fulfillment. The following are the steps to follow as you pray Jabez's prayer.

STEP 1: CULTIVATE A HEART OF SURRENDER

"Oh, that You would bless me indeed..." (1 Chronicles 4:10)

The first step in unlocking the power of the Prayer of Jabez is cultivating a heart of surrender. This prayer begins with acknowledging our utter dependence on God, recognizing that true blessings flow not from our efforts but from God's boundless grace.

To cultivate this heart of surrender, we must shed the shackles of pride and self-reliance and embrace humility before the One who holds the keys to all blessings. It is a call to relinquish control, let go of our limited perspectives, and embrace God's infinite wisdom.

As we surrender our will to God, we open ourselves to the transformative power of grace. We allow the Holy Spirit to work within us, shaping our hearts and minds in alignment with God's plan.

STEP 2: EMBRACE A MINDSET OF EXPANSION

"...and enlarge my territory..." (1 Chronicles 4:10)

The second step in praying the Prayer of Jabez is to embrace a mindset of expansion. This prayer invites us to shed the confines of our limited thinking and to embrace the boundless possibilities that lie before us.

When we utter these words, we are not merely asking for material gain or temporal possessions; instead, we are seeking an expansion of our spiritual horizons, a broadening of our understanding, and a deepening of our impact on the world around us.

This expansion mindset challenges us to dream bigger and envision a life where our influence transcends boundaries and our legacy echoes through eternity. It is a call to step out of our comfort zones, boldly pursue God's calling upon our lives, and trust in God's infinite resources.

As we embrace this mindset, we open ourselves to the limitless potential within each of us, allowing the Holy Spirit to guide us into realms of influence and impact that we could never have imagined, filling us with awe and wonder.

STEP 3: SEEK GOD'S BLESSING AND PROTECTION
"...that Your hand would be with me..." (1 Chronicles 4:10)

The third step in praying the Prayer of Jabez is to seek God's blessing and protection. This prayer recognizes that our journey through life is not one we can navigate alone; instead, it requires the guiding hand of the Almighty.

When we utter these words, we acknowledge our need for divine favor and safeguarding. We invite God's presence to accompany us, shield us from the obstacles and adversities that lie ahead, and illuminate our path with the light of His wisdom.

This step in the Prayer of Jabez is a call to faith in our Heavenly Father's unyielding love and steadfastness. It reminds us that His hand is always guiding us, and His love is always sheltering us. We are never alone, for the One who holds the universe in His hands walks with us, always present and always faithful.

As we seek God's blessing and protection, we open ourselves to the transformative power of His presence, allowing His strength to become our strength and His wisdom to guide our every step.

STEP 4: ASK FOR GOD'S GUIDANCE AND DIRECTION

"...and that You would keep me from evil..." (1 Chronicles 4:10)

The fourth step in praying the Prayer of Jabez is to ask for God's guidance and direction. This prayer acknowledges that our journey through life is fraught with temptations, pitfalls, and the ever-present allure of sin.

When we utter these words, we invite the light of Christ to illuminate our path, reveal the snares that lie ahead, and guide us toward the narrow path leading to abundant life. We acknowledge our inherent weakness and need for wisdom and discernment, which can only come from above.

This step calls us to surrender our understanding, lay aside our preconceptions and biases, and trust the Almighty's infallible guidance. It recognizes that true wisdom is not found in the fleeting philosophies of this world but in the eternal truths emanating from the Creator's heart.

As we ask for God's guidance and direction, we open ourselves to the transformative power of His wisdom. This divine wisdom has the potential to reshape our perspectives, recalibrate our priorities, and guide us toward a life of purpose and impact, filling us with hope and inspiration.

STEP 5: TRUST IN GOD'S PROVISION AND FAVOR

"...that I may not cause pain!" (1 Chronicles 4:10)

The fifth step in praying the Prayer of Jabez is to trust in God's provision and favor. This prayer acknowledges that our journey through life is not merely a solitary endeavor but one that has ripple effects, impacting the lives of those around us.

When we utter these words, we are expressing our desire to live a life that brings joy and blessing to others, a life that is a conduit of divine favor and provision. We are acknowledging that our actions, our words, and our very presence have the power to either cause pain or to bring healing and restoration.

This step calls us to surrender our self-centered tendencies, embrace a posture of service and compassion, and trust in God to meet our needs and those around us.

By placing our trust in God's provision and favor, we open ourselves to the transformative power of His generosity. His love and grace, when allowed to flow through us, have the potential to touch and transform the lives of others, filling us with hope and inspiration.

STEP 6: LIVE A LIFE OF PURPOSE AND IMPACT
"So, God granted him what he requested."
(1 Chronicles 4:10)

The sixth and final step in praying the Prayer of Jabez is to live a life of purpose and impact. This prayer is a fleeting utterance and a clarion call to embrace our divine destiny.

When we utter these words, we commit ourselves to a life of obedience, where our actions and choices align with the will of the Almighty. We declare our willingness to be vessels of His grace, conduits of His love, and ambassadors of His Kingdom.

This step calls us to live intentionally, seize every opportunity to make a lasting impact and leave a legacy that echoes through eternity. It reminds us that our lives are not mere accidents but carefully orchestrated masterpieces, each thread woven together by the hand of the Creator to create a tapestry of beauty and purpose.

As we live a life of purpose and impact, we open ourselves to the transformative power of divine calling, allowing the Spirit to work through us. We use our unique gifts and talents to further the Kingdom and bring glory to the One who fashioned us in His image.

Frequently Asked Questions about the Prayer of Jabez

You may have encountered questions or uncertainties throughout our exploration of the Prayer of Jabez. Let us address some of the most common inquiries:

IS THE PRAYER OF JABEZ A FORMULA FOR PERSONAL GAIN OR PROSPERITY?

1. The Prayer of Jabez is not a mere formula for personal gain or prosperity. Instead, it is an invitation to align our hearts and minds with God's will and seek His blessings and favor, not for selfish gain but for the furtherance of His Kingdom and the betterment of those around us.

1. **Can the Prayer of Jabez be adapted to different cultural or religious contexts?**
2. While the Prayer of Jabez is rooted in the biblical narrative, its underlying principles are humility, trust, surrender, and a desire for divine guidance. As such, the essence of this prayer can be adapted and expressed in various cultural and religious contexts, allowing individuals from diverse backgrounds to connect with its profound wisdom.
3. **How can I know if Jabez's Prayer is being answered?**

    The answer to Jabez's prayer is only sometimes immediate or tangible. Often, God's blessings and favor manifest subtly through inner transformation, renewed perspective, and a deepening sense of purpose and peace. Trust God's timing and remain steadfast in your commitment and faith.

As we conclude our exploration of the Prayer of Jabez, we are left with a powerful sense of awe and gratitude. This humble yet powerful invocation can reshape our perspectives, redefine our priorities, and propel us toward a life of purpose and impact.

The Prayer of Jabez is not merely a formulaic recitation but a transformative lifestyle, a continuous journey of growth and discovery. It reminds us that our lives are not mere accidents but carefully orchestrated masterpieces, each thread woven together by the hand of God to create a tapestry of beauty and purpose.

As we embark on the next chapter of our spiritual journey, may we carry the essence of the Prayer of Jabez within our hearts. May we be beacons of hope, vessels of grace, and ambassadors of God's love that transcends all boundaries.

Remember, the power of the Prayer lies not in the words themselves but in the depth of our commitment, the sincerity of our hearts, and the trust we place in the One who holds the universe in His hands. So, let us pray fervently, live with intention, and embrace the boundless potential that awaits us on this journey of faith, purpose, and everlasting impact.

"Remember, prayer is lifting your voice to God. Now stop and listen for His answer."

REFERENCES

[1] - https://thinke.org/blog/the-importance-of-prayer-in-our-daily-lives
[2] - https://www.christianity.com/wiki/prayer/why-is-prayer-important.html
[3] - https://christian.net/resources/the-importance-of-prayer/
[4] - https://www.thelivingepistleproject.org/prayer-not-a-monologue-by-mary/2019/8/5/prayer-is-not-a-monologue-its-a-dialogue
[5] - https://ashworth.church/sermons/dialogue-the-necessity-of-prayer/
[6] - https://opalpete.opalstacked.com/article/wade/prayer-as-a-conversation/
[7] - https://speeches.byuh.edu/devotional/the-power-of-personal-prayer
[8] - https://www.ewtn.com/catholicism/library/on-the-importance-of-personal-prayer-in-christian-life-9115
[9] - https://www.mckendree.edu/academics/scholars/issue5/king.htm
[10] - https://www.courierherald.com/opinion/prayer-is-about-building-a-relationship-with-god-church-corner/
[11] - https://www.churchofjesuschrist.org/comeuntochrist/believe/god/relationship-with-god
[12] - https://michaelincontext.com/building-relationship-with-god-through-prayer/
[13] - https://www.preaching.com/articles/the-role-of-

prayer-in-spiritual-growth-and-ministry-effectiveness/
[14] - https://witzend.me/2012/03/06/growing-spiritually-growing-through-prayer/
[15] - https://www.ibelieve.com/christian-living/harnessing-the-power-of-prayer-and-fasting-for-spiritual-growth.html
[16] - https://www.ltw.org/read/my-devotional/2022/01/aligning-with-gods-will-in-prayer
[17] - https://harvest.org/resources/devotion/aligned-with-gods-will/
[18]
- http://www.newidentitymagazine.com/grow/practical-application/prayer-the-alignment-of-our-souls-with-god/
[19] - https://christianstt.com/prayer-overcoming-temptation/
[20] - https://accountable2you.com/blog/overcoming-temptation/
[21] - https://communities.crossmap.com/t/we-can-overcome-any-temptation-or-challenge-in-life-because-god-is-on-our-side-in-this-battle/4294
[22] - https://littleprayertea.com/blogs/our-blog/unlocking-the-power-of-prayer-understanding-its-significance-in-our-lives
[23] - https://anglicanfrontiers.com/the-power-and-purpose-of-christian-prayer/
[24] - https://medium.com/@Church.org/the-role-of-prayer-requests-in-the-christian-community-6798ccf6dfac
[25] - https://guideposts.org/prayer/prayers-for-strength/10-bible-prayers-for-comfort-and-hope/
[26] - https://www.quora.com/How-can-prayer-bring-peace-or-hope-in-difficult-times
[27] - https://www.christianity.com/wiki/prayer/prayers-for-

hope.html
[28] - https://virtueofwisdom-com.medium.com/communal-prayers-personal-prayers-or-both-779974305d0a
[29] - https://www.quora.com/What-is-the-impact-of-prayer-on-a-persons-spiritual-and-physical-well-being-How-can-one-benefit-from-praying-and-having-strong-faith-in-God
[30] - https://experience-wellbeing.com/why-is-prayer-important-in-christian-spirituality/
[31] - https://www.focusonthefamily.com/faith/learning-from-the-prayer-life-of-jesus/
[32] - https://www.gcu.edu/blog/spiritual-life/weekly-devotional-jesus-and-prayer
[33] - https://www.whatthebibleteaches.com/wbt_166.htm
[34] - https://www.deborahhaddix.com/no-time-to-pray-4-strategies-for-intentional-prayer-time/
[35]
- https://thegracelifechurch.org/2022/11/16/developing-an-intentional-prayer-plan/
[36] - https://kerilynnsnyder.com/creating-a-daily-prayer-routine/
[37] - https://www.wycliffe.org/prayer/how-to-pray-scripture-back-to-god
[38] - https://www.thenivbible.com/blog/how-to-pray-scripture/
[39] - https://www.boundless.org/faith/how-to-pray-specific-scriptures-over-your-circumstances/
[40]
- https://www.bryancountynews.com/opinion/concluding-study-prayer/

[41] - https://www.quora.com/Why-is-prayer-so-important-in-the-life-of-a-follower-of-Christ
[42] - https://lifeisavaporblog.com/2020/02/28/why-prayer-is-vital-to-christian-living/
[1] - https://www.learnreligions.com/obedience-to-god-701962
[2] - https://www.gotquestions.org/obedience-to-God.html
[3] - https://lingadziccap.org/index.php/sermon/the-importance-of-obedience-to-god/
[4] - https://www.biblestudytools.com/dictionary/obedience-obey/
[5] - https://lingadziccap.org/index.php/sermon/the-importance-of-obedience-to-god/
[6] - https://www.gotquestions.org/Bible-obedience.html
[7] - https://livingontheedge.org/2017/11/10/does-love-equal-obedience/
[8] - https://www.intouch.org/read/daily-devotions/how-obedience-relates-to-love
[9] - https://multiplyingdisciples.us/love-and-obedience-exploring-the-biblical-relationship-between-the-two/
[10] - https://www.souldeepdevos.com/devotions/obedience-highest-form-worship
[11] - https://gospelproject.lifeway.com/true-worship-in-obedience/
[12] - https://faithbaptist-mv.org/d-groups/obedience-the-highest-form-of-worship/
[13] - https://www.cslewisinstitute.org/resources/the-prayer-obedience-relationship/
[14]

- https://biblehub.com/library/bounds/the_necessity_of_prayer/ix_prayer_and_obedience.htm
[15] - https://biblechurch.org/the-role-of-prayer-in-sanctification/
[16] - https://hehasyou.org/2019/12/01/obedience-to-the-holy-spirit/
[17] - https://livingbyfaithblog.com/2013/01/30/how-does-the-holy-spirit-empower-obedience/
[18] - https://www.bibleconnection.com/to-walk-in-the-spirit-is-to-obey-the-initial-promptings-of-the-spirit/
[19] - https://www.christianity.com/wiki/prayer/prayers-of-faith-pray-for-strength-in-trusting-god.html
[20] - https://www.prayerrequest.com/threads/prayer-is-not-a-substitute-for-obedience.4673914/
[21] - https://www.crosswalk.com/devotionals/your-daily-prayer/a-prayer-to-walk-in-obedience.html
[22] - https://pattiburris.com/tag/obstacles-to-obedience/
[23] - https://www.quora.com/What-are-some-of-the-obstacles-that-get-in-the-way-of-communicating-with-God
[24] - https://www.youtube.com/watch?v=gLNydJxEWNY
[25] - https://from2005toeternity.wordpress.com/2019/07/30/partial-obedience-is-still-disobedience/
[26] - https://mdharrismd.com/2016/07/11/partial-obedience/
[27] - https://sermons.faithlife.com/sermons/193269-saul-partial-obedience-is-disobedience
[28] - https://www.preparingforthekingdom.com/2020/01/how-to-overcome-spirit-of-disobedience.html
[29] - http://mbumc.org/wp-

content/uploads/2015/05/DISOBEDIENCE.pdf
[30] - https://www.quora.com/Does-God-answer-your-prayers-if-you-are-walking-in-disobedience-and-sin
[31] - https://justmythoughtsblogs.wordpress.com/2019/09/20/how-to-get-closer-to-god-daily-habits/
[32] - https://www.desiringgod.org/interviews/how-can-i-grow-in-obeying-god
[33] - https://bibletalk.tv/7-habits-of-highly-effective-christians
[34] - https://www.thegospelcoalition.org/blogs/trevin-wax/expressive-individualism-challenge-church/
[35] - https://www.christianitytoday.com/ct/2020/july-web-only/scripture-calls-churches-to-build-just-society-heres-how.html
[36] - https://www.teerhardy.com/blog/2017/10/2/unity-in-obedience
[37] - https://www.desiringgod.org/interviews/how-can-i-grow-in-obeying-god
[38] - https://georgesjournal.net/2021/04/09/following-jesus-our-obedience/
[39] - https://insight.org/resources/daily-devotional/individual/jesus-values-our-obedience1
[40] - https://watv.org/bible_word/faith-and-obedience/
[41] - https://www.cru.org/us/en/train-and-grow/spiritual-growth/beginning-with-god/the-obedience-of-faith.html
[42] - https://gracevalley.org/sermon/the-obedience-of-faith/
[1] - https://www.desiringgod.org/interviews/how-do-we-pray-in-the-spirit
[2] - https://www.evangelicalmagazine.com/article/what-is-praying-in-the-spirit-and-how-do-we-pray-in-this-way/

[3] - https://www.cslewisinstitute.org/resources/praying-in-the-spirit/
[4] - http://www.ihopkc.org/resources/blog/power-praying-spirit/
[5] - https://beautifulinjesus.com/holy-spirit-helper/
[6] - https://jesusplusnothing.com/series/post/bible-study-holy-spirit-our-helper
[7] - https://renew.org/our-father-who-is-in-heaven/
[8] - https://tabletalkmagazine.com/article/2019/03/holy-spirit-help-pray/
[9] - https://www.gotquestions.org/praying-will-of-God.html
[10] - https://truthandtidings.com/2021/01/praying-in-the-will-of-god-in-the-spirit-and-in-his-name/
[11] - https://www.cslewisinstitute.org/resources/praying-in-the-spirit/
[12] - http://theresurgencereport.com/resurgence/2010/11/01/cultivating-dependence-on-god.html
[13] - https://knitprayshare.com/blog/2019/5/30/meditating-on-gods-word
[14] - https://wordbymail.com/romans-12-2-sermon-meditate-devotion
[15] - https://openthebible.org/article/how-to-discern-promptings-from-the-holy-spirit/
[16] - https://www.churchofjesuschrist.org/study/ftsoy/2021/02/03 learning-to-recognize-the-holy-ghost?lang=eng
[17] - https://www.desiringgod.org/articles/how-to-pray-in-the-holy-spirit
[18] - https://strengthwithdignity.com/how-to-persevere-in-prayer-in-todays-world/
[19] - https://www.focusonthefamily.com/faith/intimacy-with-god-the-way-to-true-fulfillment/
[20] - https://nshorechurch.com/2023/10/09/intimacy-with-god-through-prayer-10-8-23/

[21] - https://www.mitchhorton.com/post/praying-in-tongues-increases-spiritual-sensitivity

[22] - https://christembassyhouston.org/how-to-develop-spiritual-sensitivity-and-discernment/

[23] - http://www.newidentitymagazine.com/grow/practical-application/prayer-the-alignment-of-our-souls-with-god/

[24] - https://www.cslewisinstitute.org/resources/praying-in-the-spirit/

[25] - https://thecommissionchurch.com/praying-for-spirit-empowerment/

[26] - https://www.soundcitybiblechurch.com/articles/2021/1/6/empowered-by-the-spirit

[27] - https://www.desiringgod.org/messages/praying-in-the-power-of-the-spirit

[28] - https://www.rayfowler.org/sermons/encouraged-by-the-holy-spirit/

[29] - https://chalcedon.edu/resources/articles/experiencing-the-supernatural-fullness-of-spirit-filled-living

[30] - https://www.thepassiontranslation.com/how-to-stay-continually-filled-and-overflowing-in-the-holy-spirit/

[1] - https://www.ssje.org/2014/06/06/practicing-gratitude-a-monastic-guide/

[2] - https://thelife.com/do-you-need-a-new-look-on-life

[3] - https://livingontheedge.org/2018/04/26/why-is-thanksgiving-in-prayer-so-important/

[4] - http://sermons.pastorlife.com/members/sermon.asp?USER_ID=&SERMON_ID=2906

[5] - https://livingontheedge.org/2018/04/26/why-is-thanksgiving-in-prayer-so-important/

[6] - https://thechristianmommy.com/why-giving-thanks-to-

god-is-the-key-to-joy/
[7] - https://www.karengirlfriday.com/10-scriptures-to-pray-thanking-god/
[8] - https://www.nancykaygrace.com/thanksgiving-prayers-in-the-bible/
[9] - https://livingontheedge.org/2018/04/26/why-is-thanksgiving-in-prayer-so-important/
[10] - https://medium.com/koinonia/a-true-perspective-is-the-key-to-being-thankful-168e74293382
[11] - https://www.thnks.com/blog/practice-gratitude-during-difficult-times
[12] - https://www.calm.com/blog/things-to-be-grateful-for
[13] - https://www.wikihow.com/Thank-God-for-Every-Blessing-He-Has-Given-Us
[14] - https://www.quora.com/How-do-I-show-God-that-I-am-grateful-for-the-blessings-he-is-giving-me-and-for-the-things-he-is-doing-for-me-in-my-life
[15] - https://diversushealth.org/mental-health-blog/how-to-develop-an-attitude-of-gratitude/
[16] - https://www.rosscenter.com/news/adopt-an-attitude-of-gratitude-for-better-mental-health/
[17] - https://www.reviveourhearts.com/blog/finding-peace-through-prayers-thanksgiving/
[18]
- https://www.whitmanministries.org/index.php/blog/107-thanksgiving-the-key-to-receiving-the-peace-of-god
[19] - https://livingontheedge.org/2018/04/26/why-is-thanksgiving-in-prayer-so-important/
[20] - https://www.prayerrequest.com/threads/thank-you-lord-for-the-amazing-partner.4888642/
[21] - https://proverbs31.org/read/devotions/full-

post/2023/07/26/praying-with-a-heart-of-gratitude

[22] - https://disciplestoday.org/women-today-studies-lessons-and-devotionals-item-8794-moments-of-gratitude-joyful-prayerful-and-thankful/

[23] - https://livingontheedge.org/2018/04/26/why-is-thanksgiving-in-prayer-so-important/

[24] - https://proverbs31.org/read/devotions/full-post/2019/11/25/grateful-even-for-the-storms

[25] - https://proverbs31.org/read/devotions/full-post/2023/07/26/praying-with-a-heart-of-gratitude

[26] - https://speeches.byuh.edu/devotionals/through-the-lens-of-gratitude

[1] - https://www.ssje.org/2014/06/06/practicing-gratitude-a-monastic-guide/

[2] - https://thelife.com/do-you-need-a-new-look-on-life

[3] - https://livingontheedge.org/2018/04/26/why-is-thanksgiving-in-prayer-so-important/

[4] - http://sermons.pastorlife.com/members/sermon.asp?USERID=&SERMON_ID=2906

[5] - https://livingontheedge.org/2018/04/26/why-is-thanksgiving-in-prayer-so-important/

[6] - https://thechristianmommy.com/why-giving-thanks-to-god-is-the-key-to-joy/

[7] - https://www.karengirlfriday.com/10-scriptures-to-pray-thanking-god/

[8] - https://www.nancykaygrace.com/thanksgiving-prayers-in-the-bible/

[9] - https://livingontheedge.org/2018/04/26/why-is-thanksgiving-in-prayer-so-important/

[10] - https://medium.com/koinonia/a-true-perspective-is-

the-key-to-being-thankful-168e74293382
[11] - https://www.thnks.com/blog/practice-gratitude-during-difficult-times
[12] - https://www.calm.com/blog/things-to-be-grateful-for
[13] - https://www.wikihow.com/Thank-God-for-Every-Blessing-He-Has-Given-Us
[14] - https://www.quora.com/How-do-I-show-God-that-I-am-grateful-for-the-blessings-he-is-giving-me-and-for-the-things-he-is-doing-for-me-in-my-life
[15] - https://diversushealth.org/mental-health-blog/how-to-develop-an-attitude-of-gratitude/
[16] - https://www.rosscenter.com/news/adopt-an-attitude-of-gratitude-for-better-mental-health/
[17] - https://www.reviveourhearts.com/blog/finding-peace-through-prayers-thanksgiving/
[18]
- https://www.whitmanministries.org/index.php/blog/107-thanksgiving-the-key-to-receiving-the-peace-of-god
[19] - https://livingontheedge.org/2018/04/26/why-is-thanksgiving-in-prayer-so-important/
[20] - https://www.prayerrequest.com/threads/thank-you-lord-for-the-amazing-partner.4888642/
[21] - https://proverbs31.org/read/devotions/full-post/2023/07/26/praying-with-a-heart-of-gratitude
[22] - https://disciplestoday.org/women-today-studies-lessons-and-devotionals-item-8794-moments-of-gratitude-joyful-prayerful-and-thankful/
[23] - https://livingontheedge.org/2018/04/26/why-is-thanksgiving-in-prayer-so-important/
[24] - https://proverbs31.org/read/devotions/full-post/2019/11/25/grateful-even-for-the-storms

[25] - https://proverbs31.org/read/devotions/full-post/2023/07/26/praying-with-a-heart-of-gratitude
[26] - https://speeches.byuh.edu/devotionals/through-the-lens-of-gratitude
[1] - https://www.christianity.com/wiki/christian-life/what-is-spiritual-warfare.html
[2] - https://www.linkedin.com/pulse/common-misconceptions-spiritual-warfare-ward-cushman
[3] - https://www.biblestudytools.com/bible-study/topical-studies/spiritual-warfare-lesson-1-understanding-the-battle-11554631.html
[4] - https://www.derekprince.com/radio/682
[5] - https://thecove.org/blog/the-full-armor-of-god-how-to-pray/
[6] - https://northwoods.church/book-of-prayers/armor-of-god/
[7] - https://www.worldchangers.org/Bible-Study/Articles/Prayer-A-Powerful-Weapon-in-Our-Spiritual-Arsenal
[8] - https://shawnethomas.com/2022/09/26/your-spiritual-armor-ephesians-610-20-sermon/
[9] - https://bible.org/seriespage/26-spiritual-warfare-ephesians-610-20
[10] - https://livingontheedge.org/2021/06/14/powerful-scriptures-for-spiritual-warfare/
[11] - https://www.biblestudytools.com/topical-verses/spiritual-warfare-scriptures/
[12] - https://confidentwomanco.com/2022/06/12/how-to-cultivate-a-healthy-consistent-prayer-life/
[13] - https://www.cru.org/us/en/blog/spiritual-growth/prayer/spiritual-warfare-prayer.html

www.ingramcontent.com/pod-product-compliance
Lightning Source LLC
Chambersburg PA
CBHW021457090225
21658CB00013BB/594